The Perfect
Follow-Up Method
to Get the Job

Other books by Jeffrey G. Allen, J.D., C.P.C.

HOW TO TURN AN INTERVIEW INTO A JOB
(also available on audiocassette)

FINDING THE RIGHT JOB AT MIDLIFE

THE PLACEMENT STRATEGY HANDBOOK

THE EMPLOYEE TERMINATION HANDBOOK

PLACEMENT MANAGEMENT

SURVIVING CORPORATE DOWNSIZING

THE COMPLETE Q&A JOB INTERVIEW BOOK

THE PERFECT JOB REFERENCE

JEFF ALLEN'S BEST: THE RESUME

JEFF ALLEN'S BEST: GET THE INTERVIEW

JEFF ALLEN'S BEST: WIN THE JOB

The Perfect
Follow-Up Method
to Get the Job

Jeffrey G. Allen, J.D., C.P.C.

JOHN WILEY & SONS, INC.

New York • Chichester • Brisbane • Toronto • Singapore

Library of Congress Cataloging-in-Publication Data:

Allen, Jeffrey G., 1943–
    The perfect follow-up method to get the job / by Jeffrey G. Allen.
       p. cm.
    Includes bibliographical references.
    ISBN 0-471-53407-2.—ISBN 0-471-53406-4 (pbk.)
    1. Employment interviewing. I. Title. II. Title: Follow-up.
HF5549.5.I6A46   1991
650.14—dc20   90-29176

The follow-up is the most neglected, misunderstood, and important part of winning the job.

May using these techniques win you the best one of your career.

With appreciation . . .

*To my wife, Bev;
to our daughter, Angela;
to an editor's editor, Mike Hamilton,
  who conceived the book;
to Elena Paperny,
  who assisted in preparing the manuscript for its production; and
to Sara Gilbert,
  who assisted with its research and development.*

Without you, it never would have happened.

Contents

Chapter 3: Planning the Perfect Follow-Up: Review, Record, Act!

Use different ways for different plays . . . Inner view of the interview . . . Plan timing, techniques, and style . . . The optimal strategy . . . Phone or letter? . . . Express or fax? . . . Making scorecards for it all.

Chapter 4: Perfecting Your Follow-Up Form: Respond to Get the Response You Want

Finding the words that get you to second base and beyond . . . Letters that say "Thank you," "I'm even better than you thought I was," or "I have a lot to contribute" . . . Style counts to count you in.

Chapter 5: Follow Up with References That Work: Regroup Your Resources

Review your personal and professional prefer-ence references . . . What they say makes a big difference . . . Choosing who they should be, what they say, and how they should say it . . . Using their letters and phone calls to get you in the right position.

Chapter 6: Follow Up by Phone: Recontact the Target

Who to call . . . When to call . . . What to say . . . How to use the follow-up script to get to the fol-low-up interview.

Chapter 7: Conducting Each Follow-Up Interview Perfectly: Replay to Win

You're in extra innings now, and the game is close . . . Replay is not repeat . . . How to reach the goal you want by playing the interviewer's game in the "Top Brass," the "Who Are You?" and the "What Can You Do for Us?" interview . . .

Minding your manners (and everything else) in restaurant interviews . . . Traveling as far as they want you to travel . . . Then waiting for the good news.

"You're hired"—What else do you want? More! Plus perks: expenses, company car, insurance, vacation, the right office, etc., etc., etc. . . . Cool down . . . Follow their "Yes" with a "Yes" to the job *you* want.

Get it in writing, and you're home safe . . . Job insurance policies that keep you on the team and reward you for it . . . Other ways to agree so that you can relax—after you tie up a few loose ends.

Need a final boost? Here's an eleventh "R" to make you a winner.

About the Author

Jeffrey G. Allen, J. D., C. P. C., is America's leading placement attorney and Director of the National Placement Law Center in Los Angeles. Experience as a certified placement counselor, personnel manager, and professional negotiator uniquely qualifies him to write the first book on closing techniques that will result in winning the maximum number of job offers.

Mr. Allen is the author of more bestselling books in the career field than anyone else. Among them are *How to Turn an Interview into a Job, Finding the Right Job at Midlife, The Placement Strategy Handbook, Placement Management, The Complete Q&A Job Interview Book, The Perfect Job Reference,* and the popular three-book series *Jeff Allen's Best.* He writes a nationally syndicated column entitled "Placements and the Law," conducts seminars, and is regularly featured in television, radio, and newspaper interviews.

Mr. Allen has been appointed Special Advisor to the American Employment Association, is General Counsel to the California Association of Personnel Consultants, and is nationally recognized as the foremost authority in the specialty of placement law.

The Perfect
Follow-Up Method
to Get the Job

Introduction

Why Follow Up?

Because You Want to Win the Job!

Despite over 25 years in the job-placement field, I continue to be amazed at the failure of job seekers to make full use of powerful follow-up techniques.

Studies of hiring practices consistently conclude that:

What occurs *after* the initial interview, when potential employers are weighing qualifications (and comparing them with other candidates'), determines who gets offered the job.

Yet even the most determined and best organized job seekers are likely to walk away from the initial interview saying to themselves either:

"I really did well—now all I have to do is wait for them to say 'Yes.' " *or*

"It's out of my hands—'Yes' or 'No.' I can't change their minds."

This is the thinking of interview "unhireds." If either of those lines sounds like the voice in *your* head, listen to this:

- Getting hired is still not over.
- Getting hired is still up to you.

You can predict and control every stage of the job-hunting game—through the follow-up and beyond—to seal the deal.

You wouldn't expect to get a friend by saying, "Here I am, let's be pals," and leave it at that. Or to get a spouse with only, "I'm wonderful, you're wonderful. Let's elope." Still, you may expect that an interview alone will get you hired. That expectation usually costs you the job.

The Perfect Follow-Up Method to Get the Job has no theory, philosophy, or opinion. It just shows you what works.

Even job seekers who know they *should* follow up to keep momentum in their favor tend to take actions that force them into one of four categories of failure:

- They are afraid to push, so they fade out at the finish.
- They push too hard, and thus blow themselves out of the race.
- They aim wrong, and waste their energy.
- They don't know when or how to apply the pressure.

But *you* have the winner's edge. I'll take you from the research and resume stage through that crucial first interview—then show you how to keep your momentum going until *you* say, "Yes."

The perfect follow-up *will* win the job, but developing yours to perfection requires timing and skill. It isn't easy, but it *is* fun.

I can still feel the thrill of my second placement. My *first* was getting myself hired—as a corporate recruiter. But getting someone *else* hired convinced me that:

The right person for the job is the one who can get hired.

I never viewed that second placement as "beginner's luck." No self-respecting recruiter would. They'll tell you a lot of reasons why they're successful, but luck isn't among them.

After using the ten techniques I recommend to take you through the perfect follow-up, you'll agree.

There's a systematic, consistent, predictable way for anyone to get hired—almost anywhere, for almost any job. I've tested these techniques on both sides of the hiring desk. After my start as a corporate recruiter, I spent almost a decade as a personnel manager, interviewing hopeful hirees of every age, stage, and wage. I followed their hits and strikes, homeruns and outs, wins and losses.

Look through other "career" books on the shelf and you'll see that each author suggests a different approach—and that one half contradicts the other half. Some are philosophical, others motivational, and still others personal. Judging by the number of books available on the topic, you'd think that everyone who ever got a job is an "expert" on how to get one.

Some are, some aren't. Some of their ideas work consistently, others don't—consistently. Unfortunately, you have no way of knowing the difference.

You'll see exercise books that promise you fitness *without* exercise too! Nonsense. No pain (or at least minor strain), no gain. If this approach seems too vigorous, consider the alternative: No job.

Almost getting hired doesn't count.

In 1983 I was asked by Simon & Schuster to write *How to Turn an Interview into a Job* because its president had heard how powerfully my techniques worked. Before we started, the vice president and senior editor said, "We sure can help a lot of people with this book." He was right. We sure did—probably millions by now.

Now I specialize in placement law. Thousands of recruiters contact the National Placement Law Center every year to discuss *their* placements. Thousands of job seekers call to report on their successes. Almost-rans become winners, their careers move straight ahead, their futures are assured.

"Placement" really says it all. The opening gambit is important, as are the moves that follow. But what really counts is finally getting "placed." Final, finessed follow-up is the way.

This book incorporates advice found in my other writings. It takes you through the perfect resume (which isn't "perfect" unless it gets an interview), and the "perfect" interview, which gives you the opportunity to follow up.

Step by step, *The Perfect Follow-Up Method to Get the Job* details how to:

- Decide which techniques to use.
- Use the techniques to your best advantage.
- Conduct the subsequent interviews you'll get.
- Make optimum use of references.
- Respond to the first job offer.
- Go beyond the offer to an agreement that ensures your success.

There's no nonsense, only *common* sense. It should be welcome at your stage of the job-seeking game.

You haven't given up, or you wouldn't be reading this. But you're also not in the winner's circle yet. This book will get you in shape to get you there. With it, you:

- Custom design action plans for each follow-up.
- Have scripts to follow for every stage of the game.
- Follow checklists that you can carry with you.
- Know exactly what to expect to win each point.

Think of this as a fitness workout. To make you fit for the job? No. Fit to be *hired* into a "fitting" job. Whatever your position on the career track, this expectation should get you into the running. But you can't get to the follow-up unless you get going—*now!*

Chapter

1

How Follow-Ups Make Lasting *Last* Impressions

Preview of the Perfect Plays to Win the Job

This may be the last job-placement guide you'll ever need. It scopes out the one job-hunting stage that most other guides blink at or completely overlook.

That may be why too many job hunts look like this:

- The research identifies the best target jobs.
- The resume shoots the candidate into an interview.
- The interview appears successful.

But there's no invitation for a second interview. No offer. No job.

The Perfect Follow-Up Method to Get the Job starts where others stop, because you can't leave your first interview and just stand there. You've got to have endurance. You've got to follow up.

A sports analogy is appropriate here. Job searches are athletic events—and you're a player. A *placement* player.

Everyone wants to be fit. You can work out as actively or as passively as you choose. But if you want to *win* this contest, you must *work* at it.

I'm a coach helping you with the major competition of your life. I'm shouting, "Shape up! Get the lead out! Hustle! Follow through!"

Winning in the career game takes what every competition requires a winning *attitude*.

Successful athletes everywhere know they have to play to win, and they exert extraordinary effort just to psyche themselves up. Job hunters lose when they take the "You wouldn't want to hire me, would you?" approach, yet many fail to work up a more positive attitude.

And, as in athletics, career success demands *control.*

Almost anyone can toss a ball; only a few have developed enough control to pitch consistent strikes. Most of us can break into a run; it takes timing to slide into home. At every stage of the job-hunting "game," you have far *more* control than you would in a sporting event.

Job hunting is only fun when you're winning. If you're out of work or about to be "downsized" (or if it looks like you'll be leveraged out of your current job), you *must* play to win.

No matter what your career goals or even your concern about your "career path," once you learn the skills required to win, you'll be "fit for life." Nobody can ever take them away from you.

There are two basic differences between winning at sports and winning jobs: First, in the job hunt, image is often more important than reality. A pitch has to *be* a "good" pitch—not just look like one.

But in interviewing, impressions are almost everything. They only know what *you* show. To get hired:

- Your resume counts as the *first* impression.
- The interview impression you make must be favorable.
- You must continue to impress the interviewers with your ability to do the job.

- You must create a lasting *last* impression that will "close" the placement for you.

Second, as a candidate, you have more control over every inning, every move of your career search, than you would at even the most advanced level of any sport.

There's a saying in sports:

"Sometimes you win,

Sometimes you lose,

And sometimes it rains."

Your goal for competing in this major life event is to make it *not* rain.

Believe it or not, you can perform that "miracle." All it takes is

- Control.
- A positive attitude.
- Absolute attention to every move you make.

And all that takes is what it takes in sports: *training* and *practice.*

That's what this book is for: To help you train to win the job you want. From the first resume impression through the all-important, follow-up *last* impression.

Why do I stress that "last impression?"

Consider Allen's Primary Principle of Placement:

The right person for the job is the one who gets hired.

It's the last impression that determines *who* is the "right person."

Now consider the corollary to that principle:

The "almost-right" person for the job is the one who gets to follow up.

This book's focus on the finer points of follow-up will get you from "almost" to "right" . . . right away.

Practice the follow-up techniques I recommend and you'll win the job you want. This is an easy-to-follow, proven system to get you from here to there. It begins here, with an overview of:

THE TEN "R-TECHNIQUES" OF FOLLOW-UP

What to expect from *The Perfect Follow-Up Method to Get the Job* and from *your* pursuit of the follow-up that wins the job.

"Follow-up" begins immediately after the first interview and includes:

- Obtaining subsequent interviews.
- Handling subsequent interviews successfully.
- Preparing to respond to offers.
- Responding to the best offer.
- Negotiating the best terms.

The follow-up goal is to:

- Make a lasting *last* impression.
- Take you into the homestretch.
- Make the sun shine on your game.

Whatever your previous job-seeking experience, whatever other career guides you've read, this is what you need to retrain to win.

That means you have to win every inning and score every run or you're left in the dugout.

You may have to rethink your strategy and rework your tactics. Start by using these ten "Rs":

- Review
- Record
- Respond
- Regroup
- Recontact
- Replay
- Realize
- Renegotiate
- Require
- Relax

These are the ten "Rs" to a perfect follow-up.

By practicing the exercises detailed in each chapter and section of this book, you'll become thoroughly skilled at and comfortable with each of these R-techniques.

Get ready to learn to:

Review Your Interview

This wrap-up lays the groundwork for your follow-up. Do it *immediately* after the interview, as detailed in Chapter 3.

After you've left a lasting last impression, you:

- Image the interview: Rerun it in your mind.
- Note what you've learned: Jot down names, facts, ideas to power your follow-up.

Record Your Score

You need several scorecards to keep track of all the plays and players in an energetic job-seeking game. (If you haven't been maintaining good files, that may be why you haven't gotten to the follow-up yet. Start now!) Use the forms on the following pages (see Figures 1.1 and 1.2) to record every move of your job hunt:

- Resumes
- Letters
- Phone calls
- Interviews
- Offers

Photocopy these forms if you like. Enlarge them. Reduce them to fit in your pocket or notebook. They become the playbook that gives you the winner's edge.

Respond in Writing

The follow-up letter is the single most effective post-interview technique you can use. You'll get practice (*lots* of practice) in Chapter 4, which shows how to:

- Write a follow-up letter.
- Follow the better letter format.
- Create the content carefully.
- Avoid fiddling around!

Regroup your Resources

The *right* list of personal and professional references is the key to success in securing follow-up interviews.

Figure 1.1 Career Campaign Follow-Up

Date Sent	Type of Letter (or Resume Only)	Addressee and Company	Signer	Date Called On	Results

15

Figure 1.2 Follow-Up Record

TARGET	REVIEW	RESPOND	REGROUP	RECONTACT	REPLAY	REALIZE	RENEGOTIATE	REQUIRE
Employer Interviewer	Information Style	Letter Format Date	References Who Date	Phone Who Date	Interview Who Date Result	Offer Details	Counteroffer Details	Agreement Type Date

Before leaving your very first job, you should start a file of "preference references" who are:

- Willing
- Available
- Articulate
- Credible
- Enthusiastic (about you)

Chapter 5 helps you line up this crucial follow-up team.

Recontact the Target

The follow-up telephone call is one of the most important devices in the job search—and also one of the most overlooked. Practice it as advised in Chapter 6 and you'll be able to use it, perfectly. You'll know:

- What to say, and to whom.
- How to say it.
- When to say it.

Replay—The Remaining Interviews

The second interview is almost equated with getting the job. *Almost.* Chapter 7 equips you to get from "almost" to "hired." This round *isn't* just a rerun of the first. You need to polish up your skills in all the different kinds of interview rematches:

- The "Who Are You?" interview.
- The "What Can You Do for Us?" interview.
- Mealtime interviews.
- Top-brass interviews.

Realize Your Goal

When they offer you the job, you've gotten what you want—or have you? Learn how to bite your tongue from saying "Yes" until it really is the job *you* want. Prepare yourself to make a winner's response. You'll know if an offer is on the way when you hear phrases like:

"When you start. . . ."

"Your role would be. . . ."

"It won't take you long to learn. . . ."

With the training in Chapter 8, you'll have the timing and skill to customize the position before you accept it.

Renegotiate Their Offer

What will you say "yes" to? Think about:

- Relocation
- Title
- Authority
- Politics
- Prospects

Keep this checklist in the job-hunting notebook you'll carry with you, as a reminder of what you'll say "Yes" to (laid out in Chapter 8). It should also serve as a reminder *not* to say "Yes" right away to the offers you'll get.

Require What You Want

You'll be able to accept the job with assurance once you've managed to:

- Secure a star's salary: a 10 to 20 percent increase.

- Get a written offer, or at least a letter of agreement.

- Evaluate the offer.

- Negotiate a formal employment contract.

You'll be able to manage all that by employing the techniques laid out in Chapter 9. And then you can enjoy the final "R":

Relax

The result of energetically employing the techniques detailed in *The Perfect Follow-Up Method* is *to Get the Job*. Follow them, and soon you'll be in a job that's right for you.

BE IN IT TO WIN IT

An athlete needs the right equipment to be a winner. Each chapter contains checklists, scripts, and samples for you to use to put your job-seeking plans into action. To make the most of this material, you'll need to be *actively* involved.

Equip yourself for action with:

- A portable notebook and calendar that are

    Nice looking.

    Discreet in size.

    Organized by goals, techniques, and targets.

- Planning and recording forms that are

    Copied or adapted from samples in this book.

    Neatly accessible in file drawer or notebook.

- A telephone answering machine

  With a businesslike outgoing message.
  That is accessible by remote control.

- Easy access to

  A wordprocessor or electronic typewriter.
  A photocopier.
  A FAX machine.

- High-quality personal stationery that

  Is white (or ivory) 24-pound paper.
  Has your name and address imprinted in black ink.

- Appropriate business attire such as

  For men
  - A navy blue three-piece suit
  - White dress shirts
  - A dark blue striped tie
  - Black dress shoes

  For women
  - Conservative suits
  - Tailored dresses
  - Simple jewelry
  - Low-heeled shoes

  For both
  - An attaché case that is
    - Of good quality
    - Medium size

Now you're fit for the follow-up.

But before you begin "the perfect follow-up," you need something to follow up *from*.

And before you dismiss that statement as obvious, take the time to review the next chapter. It presents the points you'll need to score if you want to get past the initial interview and into extra innings. Are you *sure* you've covered all the bases?

After you've read this book and absorbed its material, carry this chapter (or a photocopy of it) with you in your pocket or purse. It will serve as a handy reminder to guide you through each follow-up step.

Chapter

2

Warming Up to Win

Review the Exercises

$\mathbf{E}$very training session should begin with a warm-up, and this one's no exception.

Remember that "Review" is the first of the basic follow-up "Rs." So use *this* review chapter to be sure you're in shape for a successful follow-up.

As you review each checklist, keep in mind what I've stressed in each of my previous books:

Every point in the game is won through predictable, controllable moves that you can learn through practice. The easiest—and most important—element to control is your *attitude.*

The "right" attitude is the one that leads to successful *action.*

PRE-GAME PEP TALK

How's your attitude? If it needs a boost, try these words that work. I call this list the "action vocabulary." It contains the words of life's winners. If you get in the habit of using them, you'll be surprised at how thoroughly they can inject you with their vitality.

Ability	Energetic	Precise
Accelerate	Enthusiastic	Pride
Accurate	Establish	Produce
Active	Evaluate	Professional
Affect	Excel	Proficiency
Aggressive	Excellence	Provide
Analyze	Expand	Recommend
Attitude	Expedite	Reliable
Capable	Focus	Responsible
Careful	Generate	Results
Common sense	Guide	Simplify
Conceive	Implement	Skill
Conduct	Improve	Solve
Conscientious	Incisive	Streamline
Control	Initiate	Strengthen
Develop	Innovate	Success
Diplomatic	Lead	Systematic
Direct	Listen	Tactful
Discipline	Monitor	Thorough
Drive	Motivate	Train
Dynamic	Participate	Trim
Effective	Perform	Urgency
Efficiency	Persuade	Vital
Eliminate	Potential	Win

That's the winner's vocabulary. Success phrases are the winner's motivation. Here are some of my favorites:

- You never fail, you just give up.
- Work is not only the way to make a living, it's the way to make a life.
- The people who succeed are the people who look for the opportunities they want; and if they don't find them, they make them.
- We must be self-made, or never made.

- We become not only what we think, but what we do.
- As long as you stand in your own way, everything seems to be in your way.
- Procrastination is a roadblock in the path of success.
- When you try hard, you are almost there.
- We become not what we think, but what we do.
- The hardest work in life is resisting laziness.
- A glimpse of an opportunity is an opportunity wasted.
- The best investment you can make is in yourself.

If you continue to have trouble maintaining a positive attitude about yourself and your goals, you might want to try Transcendental Meditation, mental imaging, or the other techniques I describe in detail in my book *Surviving Corporate Downsizing*. You'll find additional suggestions in the "Resources" section at the back of this book.

This should help you develop the winning attitude necessary to leap from "almost-right" to "hired."

Now, take a deep breath, and get ready to get hired.

SET YOUR SIGHTS

If you've been job hunting awhile and haven't won the right job—or haven't even been able to get to the point of follow-up—it's likely you haven't focused sharply enough on your goal. You may not realize where you're going, or you may have been going about your efforts in an undisciplined fashion.

I'll lay out the plays:

- To win the job, you must stay in the game to the follow-up.
- To get to the follow-up, you must get through the first interview.

- To get to that interview, you must position yourself with the perfect resume.

- To produce that resume (and succeed at every event that follows) you must know clearly, succinctly, and positively:

  What you *can* do (experience).

  What you *want* to do (specialty).

  What your *options* are (targets).

Can you reply to these items out loud, without hesitation and in a convincing manner? Try it now.

If you can't—or if you didn't like what you heard—you need practice. It's basic; as basic as $1 + 2 = 3$.

Many people skip this critical step because they *assume* they know and can state their goals and qualifications. It sounds so simple! But don't assume. Please.

This initial workout is extremely important because, as you'll notice, it will help prepare you for the resumes and interviews that will follow.

In this section, you will:

- Check up on what you *can* do, using the *experience inventory.*

- Focus on what you *want* to do, creating your *specialty.*

- Be sure you've got the right general and specific *targets* for your search.

Begin your review with the Experience Inventory (see Figure 2.1).

Write carefully, completely, critically. Start with your employment history and *write* down every job you've held. Write the title and a simple sentence describing the function. Include volunteer and community service jobs.

Figure 2.1 Experience Inventory

From	Date	To	Job Title	Company/Organization

Figure 2.2 Individual Job Summaries: Achievements

Date: From _____ , 19_____ to _____ , 19_____ .

Company Name: _____

Address: _____

Telephone: _____

Reported to: _____

Potential references still employed there: _____

_____

Significant responsibilities: _____

_____

_____

Significant results (in descending order of importance):

1. _____

2. _____

3. _____

4. _____

5. _____

Figure 2.3   Individual Job Summaries: Enjoyments

JOB NO. _____

_____ to _____
year   year

_____
Name of Employer or Yourself

_____
Name of Job

_____
Most Enjoyable Responsibility

_____
Next Most Enjoyable Responsibility

_____
Next Most Enjoyable Responsibility

_____
Next Most Enjoyable Responsibility

_____
Next Most Enjoyable Responsibility

My own inventory began with a job scooping ice cream, and by the time it ended, I was undoubtedly the original one-minute manager. To explore all your options, be as thorough as possible.

Keep your complete job summaries (see Figures 2.2 and 2.3) in one place—a notebook or binder is handiest—and refer to them throughout your job hunt.

These forms detail your experience and help you focus on what you achieved and what you enjoyed.

Use one page for every job you've held and number them consecutively.

Then ask yourself the following questions:

- What are my primary attributes?
- What are my primary liabilities?
- Which of my past jobs (or duties within jobs) did I like most?
- Which of my achievements are sources of the greatest pride and satisfaction?
- Am I happier in a large or small organization?
- Am I a team player or do I require autonomy?
- Do I enjoy supervising and motivating others?
- Do I like to work with people or with things?
- Do I like the security of a regular salary or the incentive of a commission/bonus system?
- Do I like to travel?

While this summary of your experience is handy, it isn't really useful unless you keep in mind that:

Experience is not *what* you've done, it's what you *do* with what you've done.

To make the most of what you've done, turn your experience into a specialty. In case you think you have none, remember this:

Specializing means doing what you *like* to do.

The Experience Inventory doesn't simply ask what you've done, but what you've *enjoyed* doing.

To turn your likes into a specialty, do this: Take a blank sheet of lined paper, draw a line down the center, and head the left column "Activity" and the right column "Specialty." Then number down the left side of the page. The form should look like Figure 2.4.

In the "Activity" column, transpose the items from the previous activity sheets in order of your enjoyment of them. At this point, don't consider where you'll be going with them.

In the "Specialty" column, convert each activity into a specialty. Don't worry about this being too ambitious. Remember: You can rise above the level of your own vision. As you're doing this, your mental process will be working like this:

1. You'll select the most enjoyable activity.

2. You'll picture how you can do it on the job.

3. You'll create a specialty.

Some job seekers get this far with the exercise and talk themselves out of going for the goals they really want. They say, "It's ridiculous to call that a specialty" or "Other people can do work they want to do, but not me."

Well, let me talk you into believing that this system works. It's worked for countless candidates, and it worked for me. As I mentioned in the Introduction, I started out as a recruiter. Next, I became a personnel manager, then an attorney. Then I

Figure 2.4 Specialty Summary

Activity	Specialty
1.	
2.	
3.	
4.	
5.	
6.	
7.	
8.	
9.	
10.	
11.	
12.	
13.	
14.	
15.	
16.	
17.	
18.	
19.	
20.	

developed the specialty of placement law, and thereafter became an author in the career field.

I'm amused when people comment that I "chose" a good
legal specialty. I'd like to take the credit for it, but the fact is I
couldn't get a job when I graduated from college. Being a
commissioned recruiter (oh, excuse me, "management consultant") was my only alternative to selling vacuum cleaners
door to door.

Nevertheless, it was a start to a specialty. *Every* job is a
start to a specialty! With it, I was able to write a resume to enclose with my cover letter. Then came a personnel job, then
another, and another, each building on the one before. Then
came law school at night, a law clerk job, a law degree, the bar
exam, private practice, appointments as trade association
counsel, a call from Simon & Schuster, bestsellers, tapes, tours,
and so forth.

How many "careers" did I have? One! It's called "life." A
"job" is just a specific type of life experience; a "career" is just a
cluster of jobs.

Look at *any* successful person and you'll find someone
who has realized that *each job should be connected to the next.*
That's why abrupt "career changes" destroy so many potential
superstars. And that's why you'll be successful when you
place your career goals within the trajectory set by your inventory of experience and specialization.

That's a wide trajectory, so when you select goals to aim
for, keep these ideas in mind:

- **Set your sights too high and you'll be frustrated.**
- **Set them too low and you'll be bored.**
- **Set them according to someone else's perception and you'll be unhappy.**
- **Set them personally and realistically and success will follow naturally.**

Where will *your* goals land you? Review your inventories again, and describe the job you want. Out loud. Now.

If you've been following the exercise routine so far, that shouldn't be hard. If you're still unsure, consider this:

What *is* a job, anyway? It's just an artificial, arbitrary arrangement of tasks that someone wants done. "Creating" a job requires nothing more than creating a "want"—even a *need*—in your prospect. It's just a self-marketing activity aimed at an untapped market. Do it right, and you create more than *a* job. You create *the* job you want.

The job that fits your desires includes the place where you want to work. It's time to *target*.

Geography

Are you willing to relocate? Too many people ignore this question until it's asked in an interview. That's the least appropriate time to think of an answer!

Do you *want* to relocate? Some people just don't realize they can live anywhere they like, and that where they live makes a big difference in their life. Your area's economy may have restricted the job market, in which case you'd be better off moving.

Environment

In what *kind* of place would you like to work? Would you be happier and more productive in:

- A large company or a small one?
- A for-profit or nonprofit organization?
- A production business or a service industry?
- A high-tech operation or a creative one?

Focus on the possibilities, and aim! Now you're ready to select an *objective*. This includes the kind of job you want and where you want to do it. It includes items such as office environment, employee benefits, salary, potential, and security.

To define your career objective, list *requirements* and *preferences*—personal and professional—in order of their importance. Stating an objective clearly and specifically will guide you through to your final negotiations. See Figure 2.5 for an example.

If you have any realistic doubts about achieving your career objective, consider a simple skills tune-up: Get additional training. Take a few courses or workshops to bring up your skills. You might even enroll in a program that leads to a marketable degree or certificate.

Volunteer your way to better pay. Volunteering can boost your career because it offers an opportunity to meet influential executives and community leaders. You can develop your abilities and demonstrate them to a wide audience. An active, visible volunteer role may get you noticed in the news too.

Why not also list the ways you can *adapt* your current skills or your current job? For example:

Present Job	*Possible Jobs*
Secretary	Receptionist
	File Clerk
	Clerk Typist
	Bookkeeper
	Administrative Assistant
Purchasing Agent	Buyer
	Contract Administrator
	Traffic Manager
	Market Research Analyst
Systems Analyst	Programmer
	Programmer Analyst
	Operations Research Analyst
Accountant	Cost Accountant
	Budget Analyst
	Financial Analyst
	Actuary

Figure 2.5   Career Objective

Position Title: Manager, New Business Development; reporting to Director of Marketing or similar.

Organization Type: Service-oriented business (i.e., insurance, financial services, etc.) with minimum 1,000 employees and $30 million per year in revenues. Industry leader and innovator. Location: Mid-sized metropolitan area in Northeast, Northwest, or Great Lakes Region.

Requirements:

- Salary $65–75K.

- Employer-paid benefits, including medical, dental, disability, and life insurance.

- Environment that encourages creativity and innovation. Matrix organization with less management involvement and more staff support of new product development.

- Incentive and reward based on productivity and performance.

- Less than 25 percent travel.

Preferences:

- Minimum staff of three, including a market researcher, program analyst, and administrator.

- Sign-on bonus of at least $5,000.

- Reimbursement of relocation expenses, including commission on sale of house and interim living expenses.

These are the obvious ones, since their "possibles" are in the same "job family." What about an accountant doubling as a buyer? Why not? An understanding of mathematics, pricing, cost accounting, financial statements, and ways to "number-crunch" is essential. What about a buyer becoming a salesperson? They're just reciprocal jobs. What about a salesperson who's also a product support representative? Service follows sales. What about a product support representative who also repairs the equipment? Sales follows service, too.

AIM CAREFULLY

Now that you've targeted your search, *search your targets.* Are you familiar with *all* the possible employers for your skills within the region you've selected? You want to know who they are, what they do, and what opportunities they offer.

You haven't already thoroughly worked this part of the program unless you've taken the following actions. Hit at least five of these *directories* from your public library:

Business Periodicals Index (H. W. Wilson Company)

Dictionary of Occupational Titles

Directory of Corporate Affiliations

Directory of Executive Recruiters

Dun & Bradstreet's Million-Dollar Directory

F & S Index of Corporations and Industries

Forbes: Annual Report of American Business

Forbes 500's

Fortune 500

MacRae's Blue Book

Moody's Manuals

Moody's News Reports

Standard Directory of Advertisers

Standard & Poor's Corporation Records

Standard & Poor's Register of Corporations, Directors, and Executives

Thomas Register of American Manufacturers

U.S. Bureau of Labor Statistics: *Area Wage Surveys*

U.S. Industrial Product Directory

Value Line Investment Surveys

Wall Street Journal Index

100 Best Companies to Work for in America

While you're reading, check out *newspapers and other publications*. Business journals and the business pages of daily and specialized newspapers can suggest job opportunities, but remember, by the time such news hits print, it's likely to be outdated.

Of even less value, unfortunately, are the classified ads in these publications. Beware of believing (much less responding to) want ads unless you've learned to read between their lines, as I noted in *How to Turn an Interview into a Job*.

> The newspaper "help wanted" section appears to be an organized listing of jobs. The advertisements are in neat columns, alphabetically grouped, and often numbered by a code for the position. Unfortunately, this orderliness begins and ends in the basement print shop: it is a totally unpredictable, random, free-for-all.
>
> The only thing you can really say is that the advertisers have put their money where their mouth is—they are paying for responses. Sometimes they even want them. They may get them, they may not. Nobody knows why.

Far more valuable than the printed matter in these publications are the *editors and writers* behind the printed stories. Find their names on the publication's masthead. Since their files hold the names and numbers of most of the movers and shakers in your business, make friends with them. Two good approaches:

- Flatter them. Call on their expertise with good queries.
- Share information with them. You're a specialist too.

Remember that job hunting is a contact sport: The more contacts you make, the sooner you win. So get all you can from *professional associations and civic groups.* Whether you belong, join, or simply attend meetings, these groups (and their newsletters) are outstanding resources for your search. Find them through notices in trade journals and local papers. Look up your specialty in *The Encyclopedia of Associations* at the library. Find members in your area and talk to them. Attend a few meetings of what seem to be the most valuable groups and, whether you decide to become a member or not, make as many contacts as you can.

Your local chamber of commerce is a great source too. You don't have to own a business to attend "mixers" and make yourself known. Similarly, you can get involved in Rotary, Jaycees, and other groups that networked mercilessly long before the word was coined.

Speaking of *networks,* have you made the most of them? Networking became a buzzword in the 1970s, but networks have been "buzzing" a lot longer than that. Long before you heard the word, you were told that, in business, "It's not *what* you know, but *who* you know." Back then, it was called being "well connected." Nothing's changed but the word and the number of books written on the subject. You can and should network on every possible occasion and in every possible setting. In addition, hit the wide variety of more formalized national, regional, local, and specialized job networks. Most have meetings, resume exchanges, and newsletters that list job openings.

Use them! Use every chance you get to put yourself and your wants out there. Keep your antennae and your notebook busy.

You'll score even faster if you:

Journey to Job Fairs

These are usually held by employers in industries that suffer from labor shortages, such as nursing, data processing, and electronics. Companies that need skilled workers advertise these events in the classified ads. If your skill is in demand, you might not be having trouble finding a job. But have you found the best possible job? It's a buyer's market for your skills, and a fair becomes a self-service supermarket.

Connect at Conventions

Industry conventions are another excellent source of job leads. Attend as many as possible, even if you're only just "passively" looking. It's a great way to make contacts for future networking. Since most of the people are there to advance their careers, the environment makes them far more receptive to meeting and greeting others.

But you don't have to line up targets all by yourself. Put these professional resources on your team:

Recruit Executive Recruiters

Also known as "headhunters," these recruiters will hunt a job for *you*. Don't wait for them to call you, though. Use the networks and other resources I've just described to seek them out.

Depending on their specialty (and yours), they go by any of these titles:

- Professional recruiter
- Management recruiter
- Technical recruiter
- Executive search consultant
- Professional search consultant
- Management search consultant
- Technical search consultant

They'll charge you a fee up front, but they know *your* chosen business, profession, or industry and can coach you all the way to a win.

Seek Placement Services

If you're like most job seekers, the terms *executive recruiter, personnel consultant, placement counselor, executive search firm, "personnel service,* and *employment agency* confuse you.

Clarification: they can all help you win the job-hunting game.

Enlisting the services of *employment agencies,* which also do business as "personnel services," "placement services," and the like, won't cost you anything but well-spent time. Most earn their fees from the employer, not the applicant.

Although some agencies place only top-level managers, most work with job seekers from entry-level through middle-management. If your search is in the $30,000 annual salary range or less, true recruiters won't even talk to you—but employment agencies will.

The "consultants" (commissioned matchmakers) who work the desks at these services are among the brightest, most positive, helpful human beings in the working world. They place people more frequently than do recruiters, so they're used to handling a larger inventory of candidates and job orders.

They'll assist you confidentially if you like, and they're on your side all the way. When you win, they do too.

Seek Outplacement Services

These are a fairly new specialty developed in response to the recent restructurings in the corporate world. Initiated originally by employers, often to protect themselves against wrongful-termination lawsuits, these services have expanded out of corporate human resource departments and are now performed primarily by outside consultants.

If outplacement help is offered when you get caught in a downsize, shake-up, reduction in force (RIF), or any such corporate euphemism for "earthquake," take advantage of it! You deserve any benefit you can get from your former employer, and increasingly, these services are provided by professionals who *can* get you placed.

You see, you have plenty of resources to aid your research. Make full use of them, and you'll also see for yourself how many jobs there are out there.

You needn't *be* stuck, so don't *get* stuck. Keep moving. Momentum is important in this game, and you need to be visible. That's how you *connect* with contacts.

Don't dismiss any targets as "impossible," either. Instead, envision what you could do for them. Don't consider what jobs may be open, but:

- Where you would fit in the organization.
- What you would enjoy doing for them.
- What you would contribute to them.

- If you could create a job for yourself within that organization, what that would be.

With a little thinking along these lines, you should be able to
determine the job you want and can do, for any company,
anywhere.

This sight-setting warm-up, which you probably overlooked before, is critical to an organized job search. Now
you're in shape to hammer out the perfect resume.

RESUMES THAT SCORE

What's the best kind of resume? The one that gets you hired. In
Jeff Allen's Best: The Resume, I detail the techniques for creating
the best format, the best style, and the best content to make the
best impression. If you missed *The Resume*, read a copy. Your
resume is the tool that unlocks 90 percent of all interview
doors. It's your "paper profile on a page." It's *you* before you
walk through that door.

Is the "you" on your resume strong enough to push open
the door to an interview? It is only if it can meet all the stan-
dards on the following checklist.

Developing the Content

- Target your resume to the job.
- Start with a career summary.
- Summarize your experience, with the most recent em-
ployer and position first.
- If a strict chronological approach won't work for you,
use a "combination" approach.
- Keep it short—no more than one page.

- Put the "hook" at the top.
- List only the more recent positions.
- Be consistent in how you list.
- Watch out for "time in job" problems.
- List education last.
- Keep it concise.
- Avoid "I-ing" the reader to death.
- Begin sentences with strong *action* words that signal your effectiveness.
- Use your wonderful one page wisely.
- Emphasize *results*, not responsibilities.
- Avoid abbreviations.
- Write deliberately and edit.

Creating the Style

- Use the power of white space.
- Have your resume typeset in no smaller than 10-point size.
- Use boldface and italic fonts sparingly.
- If typewritten, make sure it's perfect.
- Print in black ink on *quality* white paper.
- Leave at least a 1-inch border all around.
- Center your name, address, and telephone number at the top.
- If space allows, include a few choice items of personal data *at the bottom.*
- Do not use all upper-case letters.

Major "Don'ts"

- Don't update or emphasize in handwritten notes.
- Don't include names of references.
- Don't state a salary.
- Don't state your objective.
- Don't give a reason for leaving previous jobs.
- Don't include a photograph.
- Don't apologize for self-perceived "weaknesses."
- Don't editorialize.
- Don't overuse "buzzwords."
- Don't reveal your age or race.
- Don't mention firings or layoffs.
- Don't be sarcastic, humorous, or patronizing.
- Don't use gimmicks to get attention.
- Don't exaggerate or mislead.
- Don't send to a personnel department with a cover letter.
- Don't send your resume in response to "blind box" ads that don't reveal the employer's identity.
- Don't use a resume-writing service.

Major "Do's"

- Get a name for the envelope.
- If advantageous, bypass human resources completely.
- Consult an expert on grammar, spelling, and punctuation.
- Emphasize individual accomplishments.

Think Marketing

- Have an objective.
- Think of the employer as a customer.
- Stress performance, not qualifications.
- Don't appear overqualified.
- Time the arrival of the resume for the most attention.
- Use overnight delivery services in special cases.
- Follow up.

Executive and Professional Resumes

- Set your goal—and organize to achieve it.
- Put yourself in the prospective employer's place.
- Adopt a market-driven approach.
- Reveal only what the employer needs and wants to know.
- Mention outside activities if they help.
- Know who will be reviewing your resume.
- Don't use unusual formats.
- Polish your resume to perfection.
- Include dates.
- Mention unusual experiences only if they'll drive up your value.
- Begin with a "power summary."
- Follow your power summary with tangible achievements.
- Give a short synopsis of previous employers' statistics.
- Edit and critique.
- Test the market.

Resumes for Science and Engineering Professions

- Pack some punch into the career summary.
- Put education first.
- Summarize your professional accomplishments in reverse chronological order.
- List certificates, licenses, and clearances.
- Include publications, honors, and awards.
- Mention professional affiliations and positions if space allows.
- Highlight foreign languages and special skills.
- Use more than one page if necessary. (Exceptions to the one-page rule are permitted here.)

Video Resumes

- Don't do it yourself.
- Simulate an interview.
- Avoid a production-line resume service.
- Prepare!
- Select a good off-camera interviewer.
- Rehearse.
- Dress the part.
- Keep it short.
- Make copies.
- Announce your arrival.
- Send your written resume with your video.
- If all else fails, use your video to improve your interview performance.

I've included some samples of "perfect" resumes (see

Figures 2.6–2.9 at the end of the chapter). Study them closely if you've had trouble getting interviews in the past, because that means you've missed some key points.

When you've created one that comes as close to perfect as possible, you're *almost* ready to send it to your target employers. All you need is a cover letter that makes it work. Use my "better letter" format. It works.

The perfect cover letter shows how your unique combination of character, skill, and experience makes you the perfect candidate for the job. (See Figure 2.10 at the end of the chapter for a winning example.) A cover letter for your resume expands and customizes it. The letter can explain an employment gap or illuminate an area of your experience to turn that printed page into an 8½ × 11-inch portrait. The more you know about a position in advance, the better your cover letter will be.

Sales, marketing, customer service, public relations, and personnel departments are the best sources of information. Even receptionists or switchboard operators can be extremely helpful if they're not too busy. Here are some questions you can ask to obtain general company information:

1. Where is the business headquartered?
2. Who owns the business?
3. How many facilities does the business have?
4. What divisions does the business have?
5. How many employees does the business have?
6. What are the main products or services of the business?
7. What markets does the business serve?
8. What are the new products or services of the business?
9. What are the annual sales of the business?
10. How long has the business been in operation?

Time the arrival of your letters, and follow up with a properly timed, scripted phone call.

These principles apply equally to all effective cover letters. In fact, they are the same for all business correspondence. Your letter is more than a "cover"—it's a package, a preview of what's inside. It gets the recipient ready to buy.

Read and remember these rules for cover letter style and content:

- Each letter should be an original—never photo-copied—signed in black ink.
- No letter should be more than one page long.
- Type each letter on a self-correcting typewriter (or word processor) with a carbon ribbon; in 12-pitch type with margins no longer than 10 and 70.
- Eliminate errors or erasures. ("White-out" is out, too.)
- Use only high-quality (personal or professional) letterhead.
- Use a block letter format. Its features are:

  Indented return address and date.

  Spaces between paragraphs.

  Double-indented complimentary closing.

  Triple-indented signature line.

- Learn all you can about the position before you write each letter.

If possible, talk to the decision maker on the telephone briefly to learn more about the position. That way, your customized cover letter will show you're custom made for the job. Your name will be remembered from the call, too.

- Target your cover letter to the decision maker.

- Address each letter completely with no abbreviations, and include the middle initial and title of the recipient.

- Use the proper spelling of all names and the correct company name. Call to check if you're not sure.

- Don't precede the decision maker's name with "Mr.," "Ms.," or "Mrs." Do use the designation in the greeting of the letter, however. (Use "Mrs." only if you're *sure* the recipient does.)

- In the greeting, don't address a decision maker by his or her first name.

- Employ a simple writing style.

There should be no compound sentences or long paragraphs. Key points in italic or boldface type are appropriate if limited to no more than a total of five.

- Limit the body of the letter to four paragraphs:

   a. The *introductory paragraph,* where the writer introduces himself or herself and mentions briefly how he or she knows you.

   b. The *value paragraph,* which describes the applicant's background and highlights his or her attributes that will benefit the target company. It's the longest paragraph, but not more than five or six sentences. It should be sincere and persuasive.

   c. The *action paragraph,* which asks the reader to read the resume enclosed and contact the applicant for an interview (or wait patiently for him or her to call).

   d. The *closing paragraph,* which expresses appreciation.

- Don't attach a cover letter to a resume going to the personnel department.

If you've read *any* of my books, you've got this last rule indelibly etched on your memory. It's in all of them. Personnel officers consider cover letter just one more piece of paper to shuffle. They're too busy to read them. The name of the writer and the gist of the contents are meaningless. At best, you've wasted the paper. At worst, you've wasted the interview.

With your resume and cover letter all set to go to the best targets, you've developed an impressive package for yourself. But this is no time to rest, even if you think your resume is "the best." You won't know that until it gets you the interviews you want.

NO-SWEAT INTERVIEWS (ALMOST)

Now you're beginning to work up a sweat. I mean that literally. Most people dread interviews and literally sweat them out.

It's unnecessary. Interviews are predictable, controllable, and (yes) fun! What could be more fun than exploring new ways to be productive, to learn, to develop your career, to make new friends?

I mapped out the game plan for *getting* interviews in *Jeff Allen's Best: Get the Interview*. If you haven't incorporated its techniques into your own strategy yet, you probably don't have interviews to follow up. So here's a condensed version:

Interview Checklist

- Schedule for success.
- Limit interviews to two hours.

- Avoid meal interviews.
- Eliminate fear of the unknown.
- Complete an application in advance.
- Deputize internal referrals.
- Wear the interview uniform.
- Carry an attaché case.
- Arrive alone.
- Arrive on time.
- Don't arrive early.
- Review your notes.
- Acclimate to your environment.
- Don't wait more than half an hour for the interviewer.
- Don't wear a coat, hat, or other outdoor clothing into the interview.
- Have your script well rehearsed.
- Use the "programmed interview system."
- Scan the script.
- Customize it to the target job.
- Customize it to your "character."
- Record and replay.
- Rehearse your delivery.
- Repeat it till it rolls off your tongue.
- Personal questions: Know the knock-out factors.
- Educational background questions: Show what you know.
- Character questions: Be careful!
- Initiative and creativity questions: Focus on what and why.

- Questions about management ability: You're an "M.B.A."
- Career objective questions: Make it clear what they hear.
- Questions about the target job: You suit it to a "T"!
- Questions about salary history and requirements: Get more!
- Experience and training questions: You've got the Experience Express card!
- "Outside interest" questions can get you *inside!*
- Your turn: Questions to ask the interviewer.
- Make the first impression the best.
- Greet the interviewer properly.
- Hone your handshake.
- Don't address the interviewer by his or her first name.
- Avoid assuming a subordinate role.
- Admire something in the interviewer's office.
- Assess the interviewer's style.
- Recognize the four basic personality types.
- Align with the interviewer.
- Attempt to sit next to the interviewer.
- "Mirror" the interviewer's body language, facial expressions, eye movement, rate of speech, tone of voice, and rate of breathing.
- Use "insider" language.
- Develop an action vocabulary.
- Write the winner's word list into your script.
- Choose and use success phrases.

- Don't use trite phrases and tired clichés.
- Withhold your resume.
- Use the "tie-down" technique (as discussed in Chapter 7) to move the interview along:

  The standard tie-down.

  The inverted tie-down.

  The internal tie-down.

  The tag-on tie-down.

- Find an area of agreement, and lead slowly and carefully to the offer.
- Be honest, not modest.
- Say positive things about your present (former) employer.
- Admire the achievements of the prospective employer.
- Be observant.

Interview "Don'ts"

- Don't smoke.
- Don't chew gum.
- Don't interrupt.
- Don't object to discriminatory questions.
- Don't look at your watch.
- Don't read any documents on the interviewer's desk.

Even if you've struck out in the interview game, these tips will make you a heavy hitter. If your review of them showed up any gaps in your training, check the lists of resources in the back of the book. Make use of them to strengthen any weak points in your skills so far.

Your goal for this round is to win the opportunity to follow through to the finals. As you check your progress, you'll see that these exercises have gotten you in good shape for this one-on-one match. You have developed a positive attitude through the development of your objectives, your resume, and your technique. You have built up a solid sense of your self and your self-worth, so that by the time of the interview, you know that the interviewer is interested in you. That winning attitude will make a winning impression during the interview.

If the interview is as close to a home run as you've ever come, it's only because your "follow-up" training has lagged. But now you're in shape to make the perfect follow-up—and win the job.

Figure 2.6

Richard M. Austin, Jr.
2441 Lakeshore Drive
Lake Forest, IL 60045
(312) 244-9152

Summary: Sixteen years of utility management with increasing responsibility, including six years in power plant process and operations, and ten years in conservation program management and marketing. Strong technical background with current record of marketing achievement.

Experience and Accomplishments

1987 to present   *Senior Marketing Analyst*
Consolidated Utilities, Chicago, Illinois

Senior staff member in corporate marketing services department responsible for forming company's competitive response and marketing strategy.

- Conducted situation analysis for CU's first marketing plan.

- Evaluated various load management technologies (e.g., cool storage, radio control devices), implemented, managed, and controlled pilot programs based on results of study.

- Key member of corporate task forces reporting to CEO and developing new business opportunities, competitive strategies, and better utilization of resources.

1986–1987   *Program Administrator, Conservation & Load Management*
Consolidated Utilities, Chicago, Illinois

Developed, managed, and controlled nationally recognized energy conservation program resulting in 5 MW of peak reduction per year. Managed annual budget of $1.5 million.

- Created, managed, and promoted successful trade ally incentive program comprised of over 1,000 distributors and manufacturers. Managed all direct mail and media advertising.

- Negotiated with contractor to provide communications, training, and fulfillment services for trade ally program and supervised all contractor activities.

1980–1986   *Energy Consultant*
Consolidated Utilities Eastern Region, Evanston, Illinois

Account executive for large commercial/industrial customers in region. Supervised all customer service, load management, and conservation activities.

Figure 2.6 Continued

- Developed and conducted numerous technical educational programs for customers (e.g., motor & motor controls, power quality, etc.)
- Won Edison Electric Institute National Writing Awards 1982, 1983, and 1984 (Honorable mention, 2nd place, 1st place) for articles I wrote describing conservation and load management programs I devised for customers.

Education: *MBA*, University of Chicago
                     B.S., Business Administration, Northern Illinois University, *magna cum laude*

References: Provided upon request, once mutual interest has been established.

Note: Ordinarily, a resume should not exceed one page in length. However, the dimensions of this book make it impossible to display the entire resume on one book page.

Figure 2.7

Daniel J. O'Keefe
25 Sunnyside Lane
Walnut Creek, California 94596
(415) 965-5418

Summary: Management Systems Analyst with ten-year successful track record in systems analysis, design, and programming for Fortune 500 client companies. Skillful problem solver with a strong foundation in computer sciences, electrical engineering, and mathematics.

Experience and Accomplishments

1985–present　　*Manager, Systems Design*
　　　　　　　　　THE BERKELEY GROUP, Oakland, California

Managed team of 20 programmers, systems designers, and computer engineers for management consulting firm with revenue of more than $10 million per year.

- Designed new systems, supervised installation and initial operation, including orientation and training of client personnel.

- Served as liaison with senior management of client firms to develop objectives, review constraints, and recommend systems design.

1980–85　　　　*Systems Analyst*
　　　　　　　　　ELECTRONIC SOLUTIONS CORP., Irvine, California

Top programmer and systems design expert with this innovative software development company.

- Led the team developing Write-Right (TM), a new word-processing program with grammar and spelling check features that has met with great market success.

- Redesigned ESC's order entry and shipping program, which resulted in 50% reduction in order-to-ship time.

Education:　　　　*M.S.*, Computer Sciences, University of California at Irvine
　　　　　　　　　　B.S.E.E., California Polytechnic Institute

Honors:　　　　　Graduated *summa cum laude*, Member *Phi Beta Kappa*

Publications:　　　Master's Thesis: "Computer Programming for IBM Mainframes: A Systems Approach" published by University Press

Special Skills and　IDMS/IDD; MVS Internals; VM Performance Tuning; Fluent
Knowledge:　　　　in Spanish

References:　　　　Provided on request, once mutual interest has been established.

60

Figure 2.8

Margaret Fuller
543 Eagle's Nest Drive
White Plains, NY 10602
(914) 987-6432

Summary: Advertising manager with eight years' in-house and agency experience with increased responsibility and scope. Idea person with proven ability to manage and lead a creative staff. Successful sales builder with media, direct-mail, point-of-purchase, and special promotions record.

Experience and Accomplishments

1987–present   *Contact Optical Centers, Greenwich, Connecticut*

Advertising manager with in-house staff of ten and annual budget of $1.25 million for 29-unit chain of optical centers grossing $25 million per year.

- Reduced media budget while significantly increasing exposure by instituting in-house agency.
- Negotiated, purchased, and installed 5-station MacIntosh Desktop Publishing network, which resulted in time and cost savings over traditional layout and typesetting while increasing in-house graphic and artistic capabilities.
- Created and controlled $.5 million promotional campaign to herald 15-unit expansion. As a result, 1st quarter sales in new stores were 10 percent ahead of projections.

1984–87   *Bronners Department Stores, Columbus, Ohio*

Advertising manager for midwestern family department store chain grossing $140 million per year.

- Increased sales 8 percent in one year as a result of intensive direct-mail campaign to credit customers.

1982–84   *Advance Advertising, Battle Creek, Michigan*

Copywriter for Famous Breakfast Foods point-of-purchase promotions. Created nationwide "Tommy the Tiger" contest, which was credited with increasing market penetration by 5 percent.

Education: B.A., Marketing, Eastern Michigan University
Continuing education courses in direct mail and sales promotion

Special Skills and Knowledge: MacIntosh *Pagemaker, Microsoft Word, MacDraw,* and *MacWrite* programs. Skilled in operating and training others.

Figure 2.9

Andrew M. Erikson
25 Hilltop Road
Birmingham, AL 35203
(205) 776-8975

Summary: Seven years as accounting supervisor and accountant with increasing responsibility and proven performance in a sophisticated computer-based accounting environment. Advanced training and successful experience in computerized accounting systems.

Experience and Accomplishments

1988–present   *Gulfstream Enterprises, Birmingham, AL*

Staff accountant reporting to Controller of $20-million oil exploration company.

- Introduced, installed, and monitored new IBM ledger system. Trained accounting staff of 12 in its use.

- Identified significant error problem and instituted new system of financial reporting to correct it.

- My efforts resulted in a reduction in time and manpower for basic accounting functions and preparation of financial reports, and annual savings of $40,000.

1983–88   *Davis Aerospace, Inc., Birmingham, AL*

Accounting Supervisor in audit department of $50 million aerospace contractor. Received increasing responsibility with exceptional results while studying evenings for degree.

- Mastered full-charge and general-ledger bookkeeping duties that led to supervision of six bookkeepers within one year.

- Instituted time- and cost-saving accounting procedures.

- Reported directly to Auditor as company's chief computer systems troubleshooter.

Education: B.S., Accounting, University of Alabama, *magna cum laude*

Special Skills: Cobol I and II programming and systems analysis

References: Provided upon request, once mutual interest has been established.

Figure 2.10 Sample Resume Cover Letter

15587 Russell Street
Greenville, South Carolina 29602

December 5, 19__

Abigail N. Hardesty
Director of Human Resources
Quality Furniture Manufacturers, Inc.
1500 Magnolia Boulevard
Charleston, South Carolina 29401

Re: Third Shift Production Manager Position

Dear Ms. Hardesty:

Your advertisement in the most recent edition of the *Sunday Star Ledger* called for a seasoned production manager to handle third shift operations at your Durham, North Carolina, plant.

The enclosed resume reflects that I am well qualified for the position, with over 25 years of furniture manufacturing experience. After graduation from high school, I began as an equipment operator and progressed through scheduling, purchasing, and inventory control to my current position as Production Manager of the first shift at Rosewood Furniture's Greenville plant. The challenge of managing Quality's much larger operation in Durham ignited my interest.

The "minimum educational requirements" specified in your ad were a Bachelors Degree, or its equivalent, in business administration or manufacturing management. When I began my career in 1964, a college education was not a prerequisite for rising through the manufacturing ranks. Through extension study and "on-the-job training," I have gained experience in all facets of the production environment. In fact, it is probably equivalent to several college degrees.

Rotating shift schedules have hampered my ability to attend sufficient night classes to earn a degree, but I have managed to accumulate 65 credits toward a Bachelor of Science in administration, with a concentration in manufacturing management, and I intend to keep working until I've completed it.

I'll telephone you within the next week to set a convenient meeting date.

Very truly yours,

Daniel D. Summers

63

Chapter

3

Planning the Perfect Follow-Up

Review, Record, Act!

The perfect follow-up depends on turning what you *know* into what you *do*.

"*The* perfect follow-up" may be misleading—not because I'm not going to tell you how to follow up perfectly, but because there isn't "the" perfect follow-up.

Different ways are used for different plays: Every batter takes a different pitch. Every job, every target employer, every job seeker (the unique *you*) calls for a different style of follow-up.

That's why planning is essential. Not just planning the campaign, but planning its *style:* planning *techniques* and *timing* to hit each of your *targets*.

Although you begin to take follow-up actions immediately after the first interview, your follow-up campaign actually begins *during* that interview. That's where you pick up the information you'll need to design the customized strategy that will lead to an offer. After all, you worked hard to get that interview; make the most of it!

INNER VIEW OF THE INTERVIEW

My previous books have coached job seekers toward success in the first interview. With good reason: the first interview is critical. It's where you make that crucial first impression. It's also where you scout the field you'll be covering to make your winning *last* impression.

Your goal for this first face-to-face encounter is to win a second one. Tell yourself beforehand that you need to come away with a good sense of the most effective techniques and timing for this target.

Then, when you're actually inside the prospective employer's office:

Be Observant

Throughout the interview, look and listen to gather information that will help you. A successful interview requires the ability to think on your feet, move in your seat, and follow the beat. Undivided attention is necessary to seize opportunities as they arise.

Take Out Your Well-Organized Notebook and Jot Down Notes

It makes you look professional. Write names, titles, buzzwords, products, and other items you can use in the follow-up stage. Don't reduce your eye contact with the interviewer; don't ask him or her to repeat anything; and don't ask how to spell something.

You can—and *should*—ask questions. Not only do the right questions help you control the interview, but by asking them, you elicit information to fuel your follow-up.

The *right* questions. Don't ask personal, controversial, or negative questions of any kind. Stay away from asking anything that will lead into sensitive areas. Invariably, salary and benefits should be avoided.

Here are examples of benign questions that have a favorable impact:

- How many employees does the company have?
- What are the company's plans for expansion?

- How many employees does the department have?
- Is the department a profit center?
- Does the department work separately from other departments?
- Are the functions of the department important to senior management?
- Is the relationship between the department and senior management favorable?
- What is the supervisor's management style?
- What is the supervisor's title?
- Who does the supervisor report to?
- Are you ready and able to hire now?
- How long will it take to make a hiring decision?
- How long has the position been open?
- How many employees have held the position in the past five years?
- Why are the former employees no longer in the position?
- How many employees have been promoted from the position in the past five years?
- What does the company consider the five most important duties of the position to be?
- What do you expect the employee you hire to accomplish?

Jot some key words and concepts from those questions and answers onto a page of the elegant small notebook you'll keep open during the interview. Use that notebook to take notes! If you never write anything down, you might not even *need* any follow-up.

Take mental notes too. Keep your antennae up and get a *feel* for the people and environment you're dealing with.

Recognize the Four Basic Personality Types

Most authorities divide people into four personality types:

Type 1: Outgoing and Direct

These people are called "socializers." They are energetic, friendly, and self-assured. To spot this personality, look for the following characteristics:

1. A flamboyant style of dress. Even in a conservative business suit, a brightly colored tie, scarf, or jewelry might be worn. Current fashion is preferred to classic styles.
2. Many pictures and personal mementos in the office.
3. A cluttered desk, or at least a covered one.
4. Not very time conscious, so you might be kept waiting. In most cases, the interviewer is juggling a hundred things at once.

These types gravitate toward personnel jobs because they're outgoing "people" people.

If you're a methodical, reserved type, you can get into trouble with interviewers of this type. You'll have to smile more, talk faster, and get to the point. They have to *like* you before they'll listen to you. And listening is not on their list.

If you're this type, be careful. You don't want to out-talk, out-smile or out-interview the interviewer!

Type 2: Self-Contained and Direct

This type is referred to as the "director." "Dictator" is more descriptive, though. These people differ from socializers because they're far more reserved and conservative. Before unconventional computer kids started running companies, it was believed you had to be like this to make top management. They're still among the high achievers in every field. Clues to this personality are:

1. A conservative, high-quality, custom-tailored wardrobe, impeccably worn.

2. A neat, organized work space. A few expensive personal desk accessories. Perhaps one or two classic picture frames containing family photos. Nothing flashy. Everything understated.

3. A firm handshake, but not much of a smile. Not as talkative as the first type. They'll size *you* up—critically—and wait for you to make your mistakes.

4. Time conscious and annoyed when others are not. Goal- and bottom-line-oriented. Believes that all work and no play is the way to spend the day.

To get along with this type, be all business. Don't waste the interviewer's time. Eliminate unnecessary words, and be sincere. This type itches around "touchy-feely" people. You won't find them saying, "Oh, I just *adore* this." You shouldn't, either.

Don't be intimidated, either. If you are, director types will sense it and reject you immediately. Don't be defensive about weaknesses in your background. Just explain them by turning them into strengths.

Type 3: Self-Contained and Indirect

Such people are called "thinkers" and might be found in analytical professions. They don't speak up, socialize, or editorialize. They go about their work quietly, and they get it done properly. Evidence of this personality includes:

1. Uninteresting, understated clothes. Gray and beige predominate. Style and looks aren't a priority, function is. This person is nothing if not practical.

2. Few personal items and "warm fuzzies."

3. This interviewer's hand will probably dangle at the end of his or her wrist. Shake it anyway—It will confirm your suspicions that he or she is a "thinker."

4. Time conscious and work oriented. Their work ethic is just as strong as the directors', but thinkers don't want to run things; they're loners.

5. An organized desk, with neatly arranged work. Maybe even a "To Do" list with half the items crossed off.

This type of person is hard to draw out and may become annoyed if you try. If you're pushy and aggressive, the thinker gets withdrawn and your offer will be withheld. Answer questions directly and succinctly. Volunteer as much information as the interviewer needs to make a decision. Thinkers thrive on data, but they need time to analyze it, so don't rush.

Type 4: Outgoing and Indirect

The most common word for this personality type is "helper." They're friendly, like socializers, but without the aggressiveness. Helpers tend to gravitate toward "human resources"; they're the closest the business world gets to providing psychiatric social work for employees.

Helpers take time to know you before the actual interview begins. They're "nice," but will do almost anything to avoid making a decision. In that area, *you* need to help *them*. You're probably talking to a helper when there is:

1. A nonthreatening appearance that matches their demeanor. Neutral shades, soft fabrics.

2. A number of personal items on the desk—often handmade. Their office will reflect that other people are important to them.

3. A friendly, expressive, and concerned approach. Helpers may apologize for keeping you waiting because they were busy solving everyone else's problems. They smile warmly, reach out to take your hand, and might never let it go.

4. A phone ringing, work piling up, and many uncompleted projects. To a helper, "people" are all that matter.

These people are the opposite of the "director" type, and they rarely play opposite each other. That's why CEOs tend to be on the top floor while personnel is in the basement. The helper never gives up trying to convince the director to "humanize," "personalize," and "realize."

To get hired, take time to establish rapport, become friends, and accentuate the importance of the "person" in "personnel." But remember to limit interviews to two hours.

With helpers, it's *your* responsibility to get your job qualifications across. If you don't, you may leave the interview with a friend but not a job. They won't ask you to give them a reason to hire you or even recommend you for a second interview. Emotionally, they don't realize that's why you're there. They think it's because you're taking a hiring survey. A helper helps, but doesn't hire.

This is a remarkably accurate way to out-stereotype the stereotypers. Some will fit the description exactly, others will fit several. No matter. Just know and play to your audience. Study the four profiles and practice typecasting a few of your friends, coworkers, and relatives. Learn to pick up on the clues to someone's *predominant* personality style. Then practice playing to them. They're your audience too!

Picking up clues from a person's appearance, speech, and body language can serve you in many ways throughout your career. In short, while you're concentrating on making a good impression, you also need to be absorbing a clear impression of everybody and everything else.

How do you accomplish this feat in a high-tension situation that must also be geared to winning a second interview? You do it the same way an athlete learns to achieve a combination of physical coordination with mental awareness of the competition: You *practice.*

Use a systematic approach. The most effective is the programmed interview technique that follows.

At first, most people are afraid they'll respond like a bionic person with a broken brain, just talking or moving out of context. Not a chance. The subconscious stores information; words and actions happen naturally when the time is right.

Practice the techniques below, as I taught in *The Complete Q&A Job Interview Book,* so your mind can focus on when and how your body is to respond.

- *Scan the script.*

  Read the questions and answers to yourself once.

- *Customize it to the target job.*

  Customize the questions where necessary to conform to the ones you'll be asked.

- *Customize it to your "character."*

  Customize the answers where necessary to use your own vocabulary and way of speaking. (Don't change the script radically, however; each answer is carefully designed and tested to score the most points. The further you deviate from it, the more you risk.)

- *Record and replay.*

Prepare a cassette for yourself containing the most difficult questions for you to answer, leaving spaces on the tape to read your answers aloud.

You can stop the tape occasionally to rehearse a particular response, but it is important to simulate an interview where the dialogue continues. Remember, there'll be no retakes in the personnel office.

- *Rehearse your delivery.*

Play the cassette at least three times a week for the next two weeks, sitting in front of a full-length mirror. Make an interviewing "set" by using a table for a desk and adding other props. Pay attention to your facial expressions, hand movements, and body language. Smile. Look the "interviewer" (you) in the eye. Try not to speak with your hands. Lean forward to make a point.

If you want to learn more about how body language can be used most effectively, pick up the paperbacks *Contact: The First Four Minutes,* by Leonard Zunin, and *Body Language,* by Julius Fast.

- *Repeat it until it rolls off your tongue.*

Use your driving, riding, or walking time to listen to the cassette and answer the questions.

You can just *think* the answers, but talking aloud to an imagined interviewer will rivet your attention. Engaging your mouth when your brain is in gear is good practice.

- *Personal questions: Know the knock-out factors.*

  Of all the categories of questions you will be asked, those pertaining to your personal and family life seem to be the most "statistical." As a result, most job seekers answer them in a "static" way, providing only "name, rank, and serial number."

  While most of the questions in this area have only marginal value in determining your qualifications to perform a specific job you must get *past* them so you can get down to business with the interviewer. That's why they're called "KO factors." Wrong answers will knock you out in Round 1; right ones will keep you in the ring for a while.

- *Take notes.*

  As you're preparing your script for the interview, practice taking fast notes too. You won't need a fancy shorthand system, but get yourself accustomed to jotting down quick scratches that will remind you of what you need to know to make your follow-up effective.

- *Rehearse your "good-bye."*

  You want the good first impression you make to last. Use what I call the Magic Four Good-bye Technique. Etch your positive image into the interviewer's mind by following these steps in precise order:

  1. Smile.
  2. Make direct eye contact.
  3. Say, "It sounds like a great opportunity . . . I look forward to hearing from you."
  4. Give a firm but gentle handshake.

REVIEW YOUR SCORE

That well-trained ending is the beginning of your follow-up actions. Start with the first "R": *Review.*

As soon as you hit the street—in your car, in a coffee shop—go over the notes you've taken and make them legible.

After mentally reviewing your performance, write down the facts. What did you learn about the job, the company? Note names of individuals, their titles, details about the organization, and anything else you can use for your follow-up letters and phone calls, second interviews, and negotiations.

This step is a major reason for leaving time between interviews. You've got to get to a quiet place—even if it's only your car—and replay the interview in your head.

Try to see yourself and the interviewer interacting. Did you assess the interviewer's style accurately, align with him, pace, and lead? Did the interviewer smile and nod his head a lot? Did you sense positive reinforcement?

Then, sit back and *image the interview.* Replay it in your head:

- Did I make a positive first impression?
- Did the interviewer and I have rapport?
- Did I use tie-downs to secure agreement?
- Did I access my action vocabulary, winner's word list, and success phrases?
- Did I thank the interviewer?
- Did my closing statement lead into the next meeting?
- Did I do anything wrong?

As you go over your mental and written notes, make some more. Jot down, now, what direction your new knowledge suggests for your next actions.

What sense of time, pace, and urgency do you get? Is the employer:

Pushing to fill a critical opening?

Browsing for candidates to file as needed?

Desperate for an expert to fix a crisis?

Gathering staff for a possible expansion?

What is the interviewer's *type?*

Socializer?

Dictator?

Thinker?

Helper?

What kind of follow-up approach seems most appropriate? You could choose:

High-tech and flashy.

Conservative and traditional.

Short and sweet.

Deep and wide ranging.

Factual and informative.

Clever and self-promotional.

You'll need to choose a technique that complements the employer's style.

Are you better off targeting yourself to a specific, narrowly defined job, or should you position yourself to creatively fill a vague gap?

Figure 3.1 Follow-Up Planning Form

TARGETS	TECHNIQUE	TIMING
		Dates to Do/Done
	Style	Letter
Company	Format	Phone
Interviewer's Name	Script	Meet

What are the target's *wants* that you can satisfy?

What are the *needs* that you can fill?

What is the time frame for both you and the target?

RECORD YOUR PROGRESS

By the time you've progressed to the interview stage, your job hunt has picked up not just speed but complexity as well.

Here's where you really learn the value of the recording forms I recommend at this stage. (See Figure 3.1 and refer back to the figures in Chapter 1.) There's no way to keep track in your head of all the activity these job-hunting techniques will generate.

As soon as possible after your interview, enter the basic facts in the appropriate columns of your charts. At this point your job-seeking log becomes more than a well-organized file of data. The records you've been filing become the game plan for your follow-up.

You need to add information that will tell you at a glance what step to take next. Add columns to cover all you need to know to make your plan.

Here's what you know: The needs, wants, time frame, and style of your target. Write them down for Target A, Target B, Target C, . . . and however many others you need as a result of your interviews.

Feel free to photocopy these forms and reduce them to fit your notebook so that you can continually keep them up to date.

Review the records of your job hunt, and you'll see you have all you need to put your follow-up plan into action.

Chapter

4

Perfecting Your Follow-Up Form

Respond to Get the Response You Want

P olishing up your last impression—making it perfect—is the point of every action you take from here on. I can't state it more clearly or directly than that.

It also doesn't get much clearer than this:

If you *don't* respond to your first interview, you *won't* get invited in for a second.

The rest is just details. But those "details" count. They count you in, or count you out.

A surprising number of job seekers count themselves out by failing to respond with even a simple thank-you letter. That lapse is not only self-defeating, it's simply rude. Put yourself in the interviewer's chair for more than a moment and you'll see why.

Your interviewer spent a lot of time sifting through resumes and fielding phone calls; arranged a busy schedule to allow for conversations with complete strangers; and spent even more time plotting out those conversations to make them in-depth research sessions. Then those complete strangers appreciated those efforts so little that they don't even bother with a thank you?

Would *you* bother to do anything more for such ungrateful characters? Unlikely.

The need for a thank you goes without saying. You need to say something else besides "thank you," however, to set yourself apart from anyone else who had the courtesy to thank the interviewer.

But what else? How? When?

Those questions get easier to answer when you remember your immediate goal—to win a second interview. That means: Impress them with the fact that you are the best person for the job.

Look up "respond" in the dictionary and you'll find that it means "to promise in return." So, in your response you want to show your "promise" as an employee—one who promises to fit the employer's needs.

That means the right kind of follow-up letter.

The right kind of letter demonstrates three things:

- That you know the rules of the game and how to play by them.
- That you can express yourself in writing (a rare talent in today's workplace).
- That you've taken the trouble to get to know your potential employer.

That means writing the *perfect* follow-up letter.

The right kind of follow-up letter to hit the target of your choice demonstrates even more about you:

You are willing and able to adapt your skills and style to the target's.

You are savvy enough to have already figured out what the target wants and needs.

That means writing the perfect follow-up letter *to fit each situation.*

OPTIMIZE YOUR OPTIONS

It also means dispatching the letter by the means most likely to get a favorable response from your potential employer. Here are your options:

Style

- Thank you.
- Thank you + "I'll call . . . ."
- Thank you + "I look forward . . . ."
- Thank you + flattery.
- Thank you + information.
- Thank you + suggestions.

Format

- Standard letter
- Nonstandard letter
- FAX
- Express mail
- E-mail
- Phone
- Mailgram
- Combination

Match the options available to the facts you've filed about your prospective employer and you optimize your opportunities to reach your goal.

A few words of caution in case you're considering using FAX, E-mail, or some other flashy form of follow-up format. If you sense an urgent need for speed, or if you've promised your interviewer some information in a hurry, then FAX, phone, or other "rush" techniques are okay. But except for a few flashy industries—or unless you've determined that the decision maker in your case is an avid gadget lover—you're better off sticking with the classic: a perfect letter. In most cases delivery by regular mail is most appropriate.

In considering other delivery systems, remember:

The FAX machine is a great convenience in many offices. It can also, however, greatly annoy many managers and executives who are inundated by the curious form of junk mail it has spawned. And you *don't* want to be associated with junk mail.

In case you think that using E-mail will demonstrate how up to the minute you are, remember that it may also tag you as an intruder in your target's system. That's hardly the last impression you want to leave!

Some books recommend responding with a mailgram to get the recipient's attention. To me, that marks you, if anything, as *old*-fashioned. Besides that, its limitations don't allow for an impressive presentation of yourself.

In making your impression, you want to create an image of yourself that sets you apart from the other candidates for the job. You want to be considered *above* the others, not as someone who stands way out in left field.

When you are selecting the most appropriate way to respond, remember that you want to elicit a *response* that keeps your action going, not a *reaction* that throws you out of the game.

A reaction is a groan, a giggle, a guffaw, an "Oh-no!" smack to the forehead.

A response is "Let's talk some more."

Here's how to get that response, as I explained in *The Perfect Job Reference.*

CONTENT THAT COUNTS

To succeed, you must send more than a glorified thank-you note. You need a "better letter."

A follow-up letter works because the interviewer is confused. There are simply too many resumes, too many candidates, and too many people in the hiring cycle to satisfy. A follow-up letter "unconfuses" the interviewer by giving him or her a reason to make a decision. It restates the areas you want to emphasize and can even change your profile completely. You can actually "re-interview" over original mistakes, underlining, highlighting, and otherwise rewriting your qualifications. Any inconsistencies disappear because your new data automatically erase the old.

The perfect follow-up letter combines the *science* of specific formats with the *art* of communication. You should reiterate your primary assets and accomplishments and convincingly describe how you can benefit the employer.

Limit your letter to one page of three to five well-written, enthusiastic, informative paragraphs. Use only high-quality stationery, and proofread each letter carefully.

Have your follow-up letters in the mail the next business day after your interview, and in your letter request a reply as soon as possible.

The properly spelled names of people you met and buzzwords familiar to the interviewer should be included carefully.

An outline for and samples of perfect follow-up letters follow (see Figures 4.1–4.4).

Perfect Follow-Up Letter, Example 1

The writer of this letter interviewed for the position of sales representative with a leading pharmaceutical manufacturer. During her interview, the sales manager suggested she lacked experience. (See Figure 4.2.)

Figure 4.1   Follow-Up Letter Outline[1]

1. Address Line

Include the full name of the interviewer, his or her full title, full company name, and full address (no abbreviations). This makes you look fully professional.

2. Subject Line

"Re: Interview for the Position of Operations Manager on June 11, 19XX"
   This gets attention and focuses on the contents of the letter.

3. Salutation

"Dear Mr. (Ms.) Lathrop:"
   "Miss" or "Mrs." should not be used unless you know the interviewer uses them. First names are not appropriate even if they were used during the interview.

4. Opening

a.   "It was a pleasure meeting with you last Tuesday to discuss the opening in the Operations Department of The Lewis Company."

b.   "I appreciated meeting with Jill Anderson and you in your office on Thursday to discuss the Marketing Analyst position at Colorado Power and Light Company."

c.   "Thanks again for your courtesy in taking the time to see me regarding the opening in Systems Communications."

5. Body

Develop something discussed during your interview in the body of the letter. Choose a topic that allows you to emphasize how your qualifications will help the employer. This will turn your follow-up into far more than a thank-you note.

a.   "From our discussion, and the fine reputation of your organization, it appears that the branch manager position would enable me to fully use my background in financial management."

b.   "I was particularly impressed with the professionalism of those I met. Quality Products Corporation appears to have the kind of environment I have been seeking."

c.   "The atmosphere at H. Price Company seems to strongly favor individual involvement, and I would undoubtedly be able to contribute significantly to its goals."

Figure 4.1   Continued

6. Closing

a.   "While I have been considering other situations, I have deferred a decision until hearing from you. Therefore, your prompt reply would be appreciated."

b.   "It's an exciting opportunity, and I'm looking forward to hearing your decision soon."

c.   "The cost accountant position and Multiflex Manufacturing Company are exactly what I have been seeking, and I hope to hear from you within the next week."

7. Complimentary Closing

"Sincerely,"
"Very truly yours,"
"Best regards,"

Figure 4.2 Perfect Follow-Up Letter, Example 1

2625 Greenfield Avenue
El Paso, Texas 79910

May 14, 19__

Steven R. Cummings
National Sales Manager
Prizm Pharmaceuticals Corporation
1050 Industrial Parkway
Jacksonville, Florida 32201

Re: Interview for the Position of Sales Representative,
    Southwest Territory, on May 9, 19__

Dear Mr. Cummings:

Thank you for your courtesy during our meeting on Tuesday. The continued success of Prizm Pharmaceuticals offers just the kind of career challenge I have been seeking.

In my former positions as both a product detailer and a sales representative for a hospital products company, I dealt extensively with the two types of clients I will encounter in the Prizm position: physicians and hospital purchasing agents.

Further, my undergraduate degree in biology combined with Prizm's training program will give me the background I need to knowledgeably discuss its products and their effectiveness. I am a "quick study," as my college and work record has shown.

I am able to travel and devote the time necessary to build this new territory for Prizm. As a lifelong resident of the Southwest, I am familiar with the territory and characteristics of the people.

I have what it takes to be a top member of your team, and I'd like to work with you to achieve your sales objectives.

I look forward to hearing from you next week.

Best regards,

Lindsey N. Crawford

Figure 4.3 Perfect Follow-Up Letter, Example 2

1250 Plains Road
Joliet, Illinois 60459

April 20, 19___

Doris C. Burnette, Chair
Search Committee
Elm City Board of Education
2040 Lincoln Avenue
Elm City, Illinois 61529

Re: Interview for principal vacancy, April 19, 19___

Dear Ms. Burnette:

It was a pleasure to meet with you and the rest of the committee last night. I particularly appreciated the time to discuss my qualifications as principal of Steiger Junior High School.

As a member of the Joliet Board of Education, I helped select the vice-principal for our high school last year. You've no doubt narrowed the field down to several qualified candidates, but there's always the question: "How do you know he or she will have the right combination of firm authority, helpfulness, and caring persuasiveness?"

Of course, you never know until someone actually occupies the position. As both an educator and a parent of junior high students, I don't just understand your concerns, I *live* them. Of paramount importance to a junior high school principal should be the task of assisting students through this developmental period with their education and self-esteem enhanced. I believe that success comes from listening to students and teachers, and from being a good manager.

This position is a critical one that affects the lives of thousands of young people in your district. Your citizens are fortunate that the decision rests with a dedicated search committee.

I look forward to hearing from you soon.

Sincerely,

James Erikson

Figure 4.4 Perfect Follow-Up Letter, Example 3

66 Parker Avenue
Bergenfeld, New Jersey 07201

July 10, 19__

Harvey D. Anderson
Director of Marketing
Fuels Division
American ChemCo, Inc.
1250 River Road
Newark, New Jersey 07601

Re: Interview for Manager of Marketing Planning, July 6, 19__ .

Dear Mr. Anderson:

Thank you for the time and attention you gave me in my interview on Thursday.

I agree that today's "manager" is a team leader who must educate and motivate his staff, then allow them to use their initiative toward achieving the desired results. Today's organizational members are highly educated, motivated, and intelligent. They perform best when "managed" indirectly.

Although my title has never been "manager," my work record demonstrates that that has been my function. In achieving results, I have influenced people at all levels across the organization. That experience qualifies me to lead and motivate the six people who will report to the Manager of Marketing Planning.

My graduate studies in management taught me the theory of management. My experience taught me the practical aspects of selecting and motivating people. This, combined with my own record as an exemplary employee, demonstrates the kind of manager I will be.

I'd like to start my career in management as the Manager of Marketing Planning in your division. I hope you'll be calling soon.

Very truly yours,

Eric T. Winslow

Perfect Follow-Up Letter, Example 2

This letter was written to the head of a committee searching for a junior high school principal. The applicant must position himself as the one perfect choice among hundreds. (See Figure 4.3.)

Perfect Follow-Up Letter, Example 3

This letter clinched the job of department manager for a man who had never held that title. (See Figure 4.4.)

Note how all three of those examples hardly even resemble thank-you letters. They're personalized, fast moving, and concise. In each letter the applicant has "connected" with the recipient; the words are read and responded to.

FORMAT THAT FITS

Whatever the content that best fits your follow-up strategy, always use the *better letter format* to express it. Remember that:

- Each letter should be an original—never send a photocopy—signed in black ink.
- No letter should be more than one page long.
- Each letter should be typed on a self-correcting typewriter (or wordprocessor) with a carbon ribbon, in 12-pitch type with margins set at 10 and 70.

Use a Block Letter Format

Its features are:

- Indented return address and date.
- Spaces between paragraphs.

- Double-indented complimentary closing.
- Triple-indented signature line.

The block format looks like Figure 4.5.

Use Impressive Personal Stationery

As I stressed in *Jeff Allen's Best: The Resume:*

> Quality, conservative letterhead will give a good impres-
> sion. Order it from a stationery printer, not an instant one.
> Use white or ivory paper, at least 24-pound weight, with a
> raised, conservative typeface in black ink.
>
> Jobgetting typefaces are the more conservative styles, such
> as Times Roman, Century Schoolbook, and Palatino. These
> are readable, available, and acceptable. They are all serif
> types ... which are considered to be traditional and
> businesslike.
>
> I recommend that you order a supply of 8½ × 11-inch sta-
> tionery and No. 10 business envelopes imprinted with your
> address in the upper left-hand corner. This is fine for your
> resume and also for letters. If you'd like to use monarch size
> stationery (7¼ × 10½ inches) for thank-you notes and cover
> letters, go right ahead. It's your money. But it isn't necessary.

TELEPHONE TECHNIQUES

Although your first follow-up response should be in writing,
the next moves in the game get played on the telephone lines.
They call you. You call them. Or both, if all goes well.
    So *make* all go well—Be prepared.

Figure 4.5   Block Letter Format

(return address)   XXXXXXXXXXXXXX
XXXXXXXXXXXXXX

(date)   XXXXXXXXXXXXXX

XXXXXXXXXXXXXXXXXX   (address)
XXXXXXXXXXXXXXXXXX
XXXXXXXXXXXXXXXXXX

Re: XXXXXXXXXXXXXXXXXXXXXXXXX

XXXXXXXXXXXXXXXXXX   (salutation)

XXXXXXXXXXXXXXXXXXXXXXXXXXXXXXXXXXXXXXXXXXXXXXXXXXXXXXX
XXXXXXXXXXXXXXXXXXXXXXXXXXXXXXXXXXXXXXXXXXXXXXXXXXXXXXX
XXXXXXXXXXXXXXXXXXXXXXXXXXXXXXXXXXXXXXXXXXXXXXXXXXXXXXX
XXXXXXXXXXXXXXXXXXXXXXXXXXXXXXXXXXXXXXXXXXXXXXXXXXXXXXX

XXXXXXXXXXXXXXXXXXXXXXXXXXXXXXXXXXXXXXXXXXXXXXXXXXXXXXX
XXXXXXXXXXXXXXXXXXXXXXXXXXXXXXXXXXXXXXXXXXXXXXXXXXXXXXX
XXXXXXXXXXXXXXXXXXXXXXXXXXXXXXXXXXXXXXXXXXXXXXXXXXXXXXX
XXXXXXXXXXXXXXXXXXXXXXXXXXXXXXXXXXXXXXXXXXXXXXXXXXXXXXX
XXXXXXXXXXXXXXXXXXXXXXXXXXXXXXXXXXXXXXXXXXXXXXXXXXXXXXX
XXXXXXXXXXXXXXXXXXXXXXXXXXXXXXXXXXXXXXXXXXXXXXXXXXXXXXX

XXXXXXXXXXXXXXXXXXXXXXXXXXXXXXXXXXXXXXXXXXXXXXXXXXXXXXX
XXXXXXXXXXXXXXXXXXXXXXXXXXXXXXXXXXXXXXXXXXXXXXXXXXXXXXX
XXXXXXXXXXXXXXXXXXXXXXXXXXXXXXXXXXXXXXXXXXXXXXXXXXXXXXX
XXXXXXXXXXXXXXXXXXXXXXXXXXXXXXXXXXXXXXXXXXXXXXXXXXXXXXX

XXXXXXXXXXXXXXXXXXXXXXXXXXXXXXXXXXXXXXXXXXXXXXXXXXXXXXX
XXXXXXXXXXXXXXXXXXXXXXXXXXXXXXXXXXXXXXXXXXXXXXXXXXXXXXX
XXXXXXXXXXXXXXXXXXXXXXXXXXXXXXXXXXXXXXXXXXXXXXXXXXXXXXX

(complimentary closing)   XXXXXXXXXXXXXX

(signature line)   XXXXXXXXXXXXXX

XXX:xxx   (typist identification)

XXXXXXXXXXX   (enclosure line)

95

Use a Telephone Answering Machine for Your Residence Phone

This is a critical step. If you're job hunting while still employed (isn't everyone?), it can be uncomfortable—and risky—to take calls at work.

If your home telephone is answered by a family member, no matter how professional his or her answer, the wrong impression is conveyed. And if *you* answer the telephone at home during the day—forget it! That telephone call will telegraph the message "Unemployed and not doing much about it" (even if you are). You might come home to a series of dial tones.

There's another reason that you don't want to pick up the phone when you're not ready. In his best-selling book *Power! How to Get It, How to Use It,* Michael Korda wrote: "The person who receives a telephone call is always in an inferior position of power to the person who placed it."

The answering machine gives you an edge. It's professional, and it lets you get back to the employer when *you're* prepared to talk. You won't get caught off guard with a telephone call from one of 50 companies that received your resumes. ("W-w-w-what's your name? *What* company? N-n-n-o, he ran away from home.")

Include your home phone number designated only as a "message number" on your resume. If you use an answering device with remote capability, return the calls the same day. Otherwise, early the next day is acceptable. The message should be recorded in your own voice, and stated pleasantly:

Hello! This is (first name, last name). I regret that I am unable to answer your call at this time. However, if you leave your name, telephone number, and a brief message at the tone, I'll return your call as soon as possible. Thank you for calling.

Don't Substitute an Answering Service for an Answering Machine

Unlike answering services, machines don't yakkety yak, don't talk back, and don't throw out papers in the trash.

Busy, time-conscious people have learned to appreciate answering machines. They're the fastest, most reliable, most consistent way to leave a message. Unlike an answering service, a machine is not subject to human error, hearing loss, or frustration. It answers just the way it should, when it should. If it doesn't, it can be replaced by a machine!

While you're waiting to send or receive that telephone call, don't just sit on the sidelines. Keep moving! You'll likely be busy with other interviews and contacts, but don't get so busy that you ignore some very important players in your campaign. The next chapter shows you how to get your VIPs ready to be ready for your replays.

5

Follow Up
with References
That Work

Regroup Your Resources

It's time to call in the first string: the power hitters. Haul the star players off the bench. Dazzle them with your secret offense. It's time to play the references—again.

If you've been following the "perfect" system from the start, you've already put some of these hitters into play. In fact, if you got into your first interview without them, congratulations! That means your target company must be really interested in you (or really desperate to fill the position).

If you haven't got the first string warming up in the bullpen by this inning, you've really got to hustle.

Ideally, you began building your lineup of references even before you began this job hunt. You should open this kind of "reference file" before you leave your very first job. Although most of us neglect this important area, it's never too late to reconnect with our past. And whatever it takes, it's worth it.

As I wrote in *The Perfect Job Reference:*

> References are among the most misunderstood, mishandled, and missed areas of the hiring process. You may be walking around under a cloud, and never even know you're drowning. What references *say* isn't as important as what they *convey.* Even such benign words as "His work performance was satisfactory." can be said in a way that will stop any job offer cold. This is tragic when you consider that favorable, credible, personal, and professional references can be easily identified, nurtured, and trained to *supercharge* you from the street into the seat.[1]

In this chapter we'll first review how to recruit and pre-pare the perfect personal and professional references. Then you'll learn how to use those "preference references" to rein-force your follow-up.

REFERENCE REVIEW

The *right* list of *personal references* is the key to success in se-curing follow-up interviews. Each should:

- Consent to give a reference about you.
- Have a surname different from yours (even if related).
- Work in an office where he or she can receive calls during business hours and can privately tell (rhymes with "sell") about you intelligently, credibly, and en-thusiastically.
- Be thoroughly prepared by you to give a knowledge-able, motivational, inspirational reference.

As you create your list of preference references (at least 50 candidates from which you should select five), look for these additional attributes:

- A successful professional life.
- A self-confident, upbeat, outgoing demeanor.
- Good oral and written communication skills.
- A fondness for you (with a little PR, if necessary).
- A desire (preferably burning) to help you succeed.

Remember, you have a *wide* field to draw from in order to pick perfect *professional references*. By only considering former supervisors or college instructors as references, most job seek-ers neglect 80 percent of the potential reference population.

Review your career history and your current business contacts for the names of influential references who can give you search security without job jeopardy. Your list might include:

- Former supervisors.
- Your boss's boss and other high-level executives at past employers who knew your contributions.
- Co-workers at present or past employers who witnessed your skills and effectiveness.
- Subordinates who can verify your management ability.
- Colleagues or others who served with you on committees or task forces.
- Members of trade associations or other professional groups who know you.
- Managers of support departments who assisted with your projects. These include managers of Human Resources, Finance, Management Information Systems, Communications, Sales, Marketing, Market Research, Purchasing, Inventory Control, and so on.
- Key employees of consulting firms and other vendors whose services were contracted by your employer and who worked with you directly. Prestigious consulting firms often have contacts—and clout—nationwide.
- Key employees of client and supplier firms.

From these lists, match the references to the target job.
For each prospective position, pick a back-up team of *specialty references*. These have special knowledge of:

- The target company.
- Influential people at the target company.
- The industry in which the company is involved.

- Influential people in that industry whose names can be used.
- The particular skills required—which you possess.

REFERENCES AS REINFORCEMENTS

At the follow-up stage of the game, references can be, if anything, even more effective than when your resume first made the rounds. You know more—much more—about your target than you first did. So you can fine tune your references to fit.

Go through your reference file and choose either:

- A new one who can hit your target from another angle . . . or
- The same one who, with small revisions, can reapproach, and reinforce, your target . . . or both.

You can have a postinterview reference letter sent to your potential employer. Or, if circumstances suit, your reference can telephone the target.

LINE UP THE DEFENSE

No matter how you plan to play your references, follow *protocol*. (It's not just polite. It's the only way to win.)

When you *intend* to give a reference's name to an interviewer, or at the *very* latest, as soon as you have, inform the reference of that fact! Provide information about:

Who may be calling.

From what company.

About what position.

Suggest a focus for the conversation that makes *this* reference the perfect backup for *this* position.

Remind your references of the material you've provided them to be sure they're warmed up to make the perfect response.

When you're following up with your best follow-up references, be sure that each has—and is familiar with—the following items that make up your *"preference reference"* packet:

- A sample completed application. (Applications are available from employers by calling and asking for them to be mailed. Stationery stores also have ones you can buy.)

- Your resume. (Only a *super-resume* will do. See *Jeff Allen's Best: The Resume*.)

- Your individual "reference summary."

- A reference questions list.

Samples of the last two items are shown in Figures 5.1 through 5.4, one for professional references, and a different one for personal references. Prepare a summary and question list for each reference, and keep copies for *your* reference during interviews.

The Professional Reference Summary

This is a brief, neatly typed, one-page summary that reviews significant facts about you and your record. Concentrate on traits, skills, and accomplishments that apply to target jobs.

The Professional Reference Questions List

The final item you will give each reference is two versions of a list of questions that reference is likely to be asked in a telephone reference check. The first will have "suggested" answers

Figure 5.1 The Professional Reference Summary

Name: John R. Smith   Tel No.: (917) 321-8732

Former Title: National Sales Manager

Accomplishments

- Supervised and motivated a field sales force that grew from 12 people to 20 during three-year tenure. Managed and led in-house sales support staff of six.

- Set and monitored sales objectives by territory and product, resulting in an average annual increase in sales of 30 percent, with an overall three-year cumulative increase of 120 percent (from $6 million in 1980 to $13.2 million in 1983).

- Purchased and installed computerized sales monitoring and reporting system.

- Used customer feedback to help create and market three new products—the Accu Soft, the Accu Sort, and the Accu Scan—which are consistently among the top sellers produced by the company.

- Established a sales incentive program that increased sales across the board and more than 50 percent in each of the two lowest performing territories.

  Traits: • Fast moving, effective, results oriented.
          • Highly skilled at motivating others to achieve their goals.
          • Reliable, loyal, enthusiastic.

Figure 5.2   The Professional Reference Questions List

How long have you known _____ ?

How do you know _____ ?

When was he/she hired? _____

When did he/she leave? _____

What was his/her salary when he/she left? _____

Why did he/she leave? _____

Did you work with him/her directly? _____

Was he usually on time? _____

Was he/she absent from work very often? _____

Did his/her personal life ever interfere with his/her work? _____

What were his/her titles? _____

What were his/her duties? _____

Did he/she cooperate with supervisors? _____

Did he/she cooperate with coworkers? _____

Did he/she take work home very often? _____

What are his/her primary attributes? _____

What are his/her primary liabilities? _____

Is he/she eligible for rehire? _____

Can you confirm the information he/she has given? _____

Figure 5.3 The Personal Reference Summary

Name: Betty R. Brown   Telephone No. (616) 522-3359

Position Desired: Accountant, Insurance Company

Character Traits

- Determination

- Accuracy

- Thoroughness

- Commitment

- Follow through

- Energy

- Enthusiasm

- Competence

- Positive attitude

Job-Related Abilities and Skills

- Compiled financial data and developed complete, accurate forecasts.

- Presented concise, understandable financial reports for budget projections.

- Knowledge of accounting principles and procedures.

Figure 5.4 The Personal Reference Questions List

How long have you known _____ ?

How do you know _____ ?

_____

What is your opinion of _____ ?

_____

_____

_____

Does he/she get along well with others? _____

Is he/she usually on time? _____

Is he/she absent from work very often? _____

Does he/she bring work home very often? _____

Does he/she like his/her job? _____

What are his/her primary attributes? _____

_____

_____

_____

What are his/her primary liabilities? _____

_____

_____

_____

_____

completed by you. This helps the reference "remember." Give all of your references copies of the blank list too, so they at least feel they have the opportunity to answer it in their own words.

The Personal Reference Summary

This is a one-page summary or list that describes attributes that the reference can authenticate and are relevant to your target job.

The Personal Reference Questions List

The final item to give your references is a duplicate list of questions they are likely to be asked by a reference checker. The first copy will have "suggested" answers written by you. The second copy of the list you provide will be blank to allow your references to use the information you have given and their own recall to create their own responses.

GO ON THE OFFENSE

You needn't wait for your employers to call before you put your references into the game. Those specialized preference references can write or phone the prospect to give *your* prospects a boost. Here's how.

Letters That Lock in the Target

As I wrote in *The Perfect Job Reference*, a second, postinterview letter must be:

A super-reference, *written by* the right person, *targeted* to the right person (a decision-maker), and containing marketable information about your abilities and skills. What someone else says about you has ten times the influence of what you say about yourself.

Use a brief, perfectly drafted one-page letter—from a carefully selected reference as a *cover letter* for your resume. Personalize each letter to individuals inside the target company(ies) who either have:

- The authority to hire you, or
- Connections to those who do.[2]

The key is *positioning*.

The position of your reference, the way you are positioned by your reference in a letter or telephone call, targeting a specific position, and someone in a position to hire for it are all essential elements of a super-reference.

To position yourself for the perfect position, choose a reference who is in the best position to write the best positioning letter for you.

Who Should Write

As I suggested in *The Perfect Job Reference,*

Selection of the reference cover letter writer is the first element of positioning. He or she should be:

- Someone who knows the recipient of the letter.
- Someone who knows someone else the recipient knows.
- Someone who, by reputation, is known to the recipient of the letter.
- Someone whose letterhead, title, and responsibil-

ities will attract the recipient's attention or give credibility to the statements in the letter—and to you.

The writer of the reference cover letter should hold an equal or superior position to the recipient. An exception might be when the letter is written from a former employee who left in good standing.[3]

Pick Your Best Target

Ask your references for suggestions of people who are in the best position to help you. Why? Consider this case from *The Perfect Job Reference:*

> Judy was stalled in her job as a writer of programming manuals for a small East Coast software manufacturer. She had been with the company for three years and had been promoted to supervisor of her department of four writers and a technical editor.
>
> Although her undergraduate degree was in computer science, she studied at night to complete an MBA with an emphasis in marketing. Judy believed that her education, combined with her knowledge of user needs, prepared her for a marketing manager position. But her company had only one such position, and it didn't look like it would be vacant soon.
>
> So, Judy decided to review her contacts to find a few superstars who could become super-references.
>
> She decided on:
>
> "Judd," a former coworker, who left to start a small software company. Although Judd's company only had a few products, one of them had recently been successful and was getting loads of industry attention. Judd's letterhead read "Justin Davis, President, Specialized Software Corporation" with a prestigious Los Angeles address.

Then there was "Elizabeth," a marketing manager of computer peripherals whom Judy had met at a conference; and

"Dr. William Dutton," an adjunct faculty member at the graduate school of business where Judy had studied, a former government official, and the director of competitive intelligence for a defense manufacturing company. Judy took Dr. Dutton's course in competitive intelligence and business marketing. They became friends and she even helped him prepare a manuscript.

Judy's three principal references had a wealth of contacts in the software marketing business who could help her target marketing directors of manufacturers. The letters they wrote to introduce her and direct attention to her resume won her interview after interview. She had four reference-influenced offers, and today she's rapidly climbing the marketing ladder at one of the world's biggest software manufacturers.[4]

Your story can be just as simple as Judy's, its ending just as sweet. Even if you don't know any highly placed officials or company presidents, *somewhere* among your professional and personal contacts is one person (and another, and another) who can reinforce the good impression you made on your target.

Help Them Say the Right Thing

Most references simply haven't a clue when it comes to writing the perfect letter. That's why typical reference letters are ridiculous. References aren't particularly good learners, either. After all, if they weren't more important than you, you wouldn't need them to lend you their importance, right? It's not only *their* belief—it's yours.

So, rather than try to teach them or leave the letters' impact to chance, *write your perfect letters yourself*! The result is a far more detailed, consistent presentation, and your references will probably be relieved.

Just ask. You'll probably hear: "Sure, whatever you want. Just type it up and I'll sign it."

If a reference does want to take full responsibility for the letter, at the very least give him or her the better letter formats and examples from this chapter and ask that they be followed as closely as possible.

If the reference is a personal friend or colleague well known to the target, the opening and closing paragraphs should be in the writer's own words. But you can help by supplying the language for the value paragraph.

You can also provide the information you want conveyed by adding to your Professional and Personal Reference Summaries (see Figures 5.1–5.4) a section that lists the traits, accomplishments, and skills that make you perfect for each particular job.

The resulting letters should be like the samples shown in Figures 5.5 and 5.6. They can make you a winner.

Now some cheerleading is in order. When you let your references know of the impending reference check, let them in on your excitement too. After the usual affable greetings, announce: "I hope you'll be as pleased as I am to know that I'm close to getting that job I mentioned at XYZ Company. It looks like a *really* good deal, and I think it will be a terrific opportunity for me! And *you* may be the one who could help me land it!"

Fill your by-now-enthusiastic teammate in on what you've learned from the interview and what kind of call he or she can expect, from what kind of person.

Don't coach your references so well that they sound "canned," but do be sure that each one understands:

Figure 5.5   Sample Reference Letter

Employers Insurance Companies
Corporate Headquarters
One Founders Plaza
Hartford, Connecticut 06210
(203) 526-0100

Henry V. Tattersall III
Chief Financial Officer

January 15, 19___

Edgar O. Winston
Chief Financial Officer
General Investors Group
1200 Park Avenue
New York, New York 10011

Re: Joel M. Adams Reference

Dear Mr. Winston:

As chief financial officers of multinational companies, you and I know how important the internal audit process is to our financial stability. But talented, skilled, effective audit managers are almost impossible to find.

My associate, Joel Adams, is one of them. A 20-year veteran of multinational audit management with direct responsibility to the CFO, Mr. Adams uses his keen understanding of the audit process to develop solutions to complex financial problems. His enclosed resume will illuminate his record at Wharton and his ability as an audit manager.

Mr. Adams reported directly to me in my former position as CFO at Amalgamated Industries. I'm glad you've had the opportunity to speak with him, and I'm sure that by now you can see for yourself how much you could benefit from his expertise as a highly qualified audit manager.

If you would like any further information from me about Joel Adams, please do not hesitate to call.

Sincerely,

Henry V. Tattersall III

HVT:meg

Enclosure: Joel M. Adams resume

Figure 5.6 Sample Reference Letter

American Foods Company
2204 Mercantile Building
Chicago, Illinois 60626
(312) 974-0700

Angela P. Edwards, Director
Market Research

April 3, 19___

Margaret O. Blaine, Product Manager
Convenience Foods Division
American Foods Company
1667 Commonwealth Avenue
Boston, MA 02210

Re: Amanda F. Harston Reference

Dear Marge:

I hope all is going well with your new product launch. Last November, when my department gave you that revised market research you needed, you asked me to let you know if you could return the favor. Well, now you can.

My associate and friend, Amanda Harston, is applying for the assistant product manager position that opened at the breakfast division of American. In addition to great credentials, Amanda has the energy, insight, and dedication needed to be an outstanding assistant product manager.

As the enclosed resume shows, Amanda recently enhanced her ten years' experience in product marketing at XYZ, Inc., with an MBA from Bentley College. She graduated with high honors in spite of a 60-hour-a-week job that required 70 percent travel time. Although she has moved up steadily at XYZ, now that she has solid experience and graduate credentials, she'd like a larger environment.

I know that John Lawson, who is hiring for this position, has interviewed Amanda. I hope you'll let him know that an even closer look won't be a waste of time. In fact, John will probably feel he owes you a favor once he meets Amanda.

If you'd like me to fill you in on why he would benefit from another talk with her, just let me know. I'd love to hear from you!

Best regards,

Angela P. Edwards

APE:sae
Enclosure: Amanda Harston resume

- The objectives of your job search.

- The specific knowledge that you'd like him or her to relate in a reference call.

- The delivery necessary for maximum impact on the reference checker.

Ask your references to accept the telephone calls or return them immediately (you'll pay any toll charges), and to notify you of the details the moment they hang up. You need the feedback and you need it fast.

Finally, arrange for some follow-up of your own.

GETTING PERSONAL

You can really reap benefits from this kind of "personal" touch if one or more of your preference references—professional as well as personal—knows a contact at your prime target well enough to put in a good word for you by *telephone*.

You prepare them to do this big favor for you by following all the preceding techniques. For a "script" they can use the kinds of words used in the sample letters (Figures 5.5 and 5.6). Just keep in mind that this *is* a big favor—one you can ask for only once. Choose carefully and proceed delicately.

No matter who they are or how they're used, references can indeed be the power players in your follow-up bid. But once you play them, they're out of your hands. That's why you prep them so fully. And it's because of their power, in this follow-up and future ones, that you never treat them any way but well.

Always recontact your references after they've made their play in your behalf to:

- Express your gratitude and appreciation.
- Ask about their impression of your prospective employer—and your prospects.
- Express your gratitude and appreciation. Again.

This exercise in politeness is not intended simply to display your good manners. It's to prepare you for your own next step. After your reference reinforcement, it's time for *you* to recontact the prospect. Take a deep breath!

Chapter

6

Follow Up by Phone

Recontact the Target

You're headed for the pennant. You've played the perfect letter. You've got a team of references cheering you on. You might think you could coast a little now. But not if you want to finish in the finals.

I promised this would be a vigorous workout; but even if you, like most smart and winning job seekers, are playing at your peak and feeling a bit breathless, get ready for a second wind.

Because now it's time for the Perfect Follow-Up phone call.

If the very thought of that makes you clutch, keep in mind that this very professional play (or ploy) will put you way ahead of the pack. And relax; by the time you've studied and practiced this chapter, you'll be able to do it without a fumble.

I've said it before, but it bears repeating:

The follow-up telephone call is one of the most important devices in the job search—and also one of the most unused.

As important as it was in the follow-up to your resume, it's at least as important in following up your first interview—and moving to your second. This time it will be easier, because you learned some new topics of conversation during your first interview.

As with your initial follow-up response, the keys to success when you telephone your target are timing and technique. That means knowing:

- When to call.
- Whom to call.
- What to say.

Your ongoing purpose is to maintain the prospect's impression of you as:

- Enthusiastic.
- Confident.
- Energetic.
- Dependable.
- Loyal.
- Honest.
- Proud of your work.
- Concerned with service.

The fact that you're taking the trouble to make this follow-up call can, by itself, demonstrate these qualities.

If you feel any qualms, just remember your goal: an interview replay that makes you a winner.

TIMING THE TELEPHONE FOLLOW-UP

Don't Wait Too Long

The best advice to heed is the "fiddle theory," introduced by Robert Ringer in *Winning Through Intimidation*:

> The longer a person fiddles around with something, the greater the odds that the result will be negative. . . . In the

case of Nero, Rome burned; in the case of a sale, the longer it takes to get to a point of closing, the greater the odds it will never close.

As a general rule, you should assume that time is always against you when you try to make a deal—any kind of deal. There's an old saying about "striking while the iron's hot," and my experience has taught me that it certainly is a profound statement in that circumstances always seem to have a way of changing.[1]

If you haven't received a response to your follow-up letter *within a week* after the interview, call.

Never on a Monday

Mondays are full of staff meetings, unexpected crises, and weekend wounds. Don't call, write, or interview on a Monday if you can help it.

Statistically, the *best* time to call is Tuesday through Friday, from 9:00 A.M. to 11:00 A.M.

TARGETING THE TELEPHONE FOLLOW-UP

You already know *who* should receive your call. You spent a long time talking with him or her during your first interview. Despite my interview tips, you may still feel in a one-down position with your interviewer. Don't.

Initiating the call automatically gives you the upper hand. You're prepared and can guide the conversation to the outcome you want.

This means that *waiting* for a call can push your foot out of the interviewer's door. It's up to you. What will it be? "Don't call us, we'll call you," or "Please call us, we're too (busy, disorganized, confused, etc.) to call you."?

That's exactly what I did to get the best job of my career. I took a deep breath and called the vice president and general counsel of a major bank. He was in charge of hiring for the position I wanted. Here's how I described the experience in *The Perfect Job Reference*:

JGA: (Deep breath) Hello, Mr. _____ . This is Jeff Allen. I'm calling to thank you for interviewing me for the legal assistant position.

AMR: (In a hurried, distracted tone) Right. I have your resume on the pile in front of me. I'm glad you called! That's one less decision I have to make. You've got the job. Start the first of the month.

Talk about acceptance shock! It was all I could do to keep from running over to my boss and giving notice. I called the personnel office at least a dozen times with creative questions just to be sure I hadn't been dreaming (an occupational hazard for night law students with day jobs).

When *you* make the phone call, sounding confident and assured, you really *are* in control. You have the facts about the best possible candidate—you—immediately available. You have a second, critical chance to emphasize your professionalism, confidence, and job skills. AMR didn't stand a chance; on my start date he confessed he couldn't even remember who I *was*![2]

If your timing is right, your target will be reviewing resumes when you call. You're the only candidate with a persuasive, intelligent spokesperson on the line at the moment, and therefore you improve your chances dramatically.

If you call very early (before 9:00 A.M.) or late (after 5:00 P.M.), you can often hit your target directly. But if you do need to get past a gatekeeper to reach your target, having been interviewed makes it easier, since it provides a credible reason to call.

Should you have trouble, remember to treat the executive's secretary or assistant as your ally, not your adversary. Don't play games to get around the front desk: Businesspeople use their names and state the purpose of their calls. Don't ask annoying questions about the boss's schedule, hoping to catch him or her unguarded. Instead, use a courteous, firm tone of voice and follow a script like this if you speak to the secretary:

Secretary: Good morning, Mr. Wagner's office.

You: This is Donna Boardman calling. May I speak to him, please?

Secretary: I'm sorry, he's away from his desk/on another line/in a meeting. May I take a message?

You: Mr. Wagner and I met last week regarding the engineering manager position.

Secretary: One minute please.

The boss might very well be away from his desk, on another line, or in a meeting. But probably the secretary is checking to see whether he wants to take the call. If not:

You: When would be a good time to call him back? (or) I'll hold on, if it won't tie up your line.

Since you have been direct and cooperative, the secretary is inclined to return the courtesy. Also be polite and stubborn: you'll get through before long.[3]

PRACTICE, PRACTICE, PRACTICE

When you do get through, you'll sound like a winner. As I mentioned to telephobic job seekers in *How to Turn an Interview into a Job*:

> I know you think the interviewer will be angry at you, and you therefore will not be hired. It's like calling your first blind date. But the reality is that you are just replaying old memories.
>
> The *fact* is that, unless the interviewer has said something like:
>
> "I *never* want to hear from you again!" or
> "If you phone me, I guarantee you *won't* get this job!" (neither of which is likely), a phone call at least can't hurt you.
>
> More likely, it can help you. It can restate your image at the most crucial stage of the hirer's consideration process: the postinterview evaluation.
>
> You can control this interaction too. Practice![4]

PERFECT YOUR DELIVERY

Do you really know how you sound to others on the phone? Do you come across assertively, confidently, and professionally? Do you sound interesting? Would *you* hire you? If you don't know, find out. Before you talk to others, pick up the handset and talk to yourself.

That answering machine I recommended serves a dual purpose. Use it to perfect your delivery. Prepare a script based on the suggestions that follow for the "deep-breath phone call" or the "consultant phone call." Then sit down at another telephone (in a phone booth if you have to), call yourself up, and record your conversation. It's helpful to have a friend waiting for your call to act as an interviewer. Either way, be sure the call is recorded on your machine. When you play back your recording, evaluate the content and style.

Let's talk about content first. Are your words appropriate to your audience? Trade "buzzwords" and language unique to your field should be saved for the departmental hiring authority; keep your conversations with human resourcers simple. If they get confused, they won't invite you for an interview, because they don't want you to know they're out of their depth.

Make sure your words carry authority and authenticity. Convey to the listener that you know what you're talking about without reading a telemarketing script. Don't bang your gums on the interviewer's drums. Motor-mouths get tired before they're hired.

Make sure you sound *clear*. Don't slur. Eliminate extra words and phrases. Get rid of "ah," "y'know," "like," and other audible pauses.

Under pressure, some people skip back to repetitive openers like a broken record. If you find yourself saying, "As I said," "Needless to say," or "Given this," stop. It's a verbal tick that's as annoying to hear as a facial one is to watch.

Do you talk too fast to be understood? Slow down. Is your speech already slow enough to make a sleepwalking staffer snore? Discipline yourself to deliver with an even tone and moderate pace.

Practice, record, listen, then practice again until you've eliminated any speech patterns that steer you away from clear, direct, one-to-one communication.

ATTACH A MIRROR TO YOUR TELEPHONE

Did you ever catch yourself in a mirror with a glum look, sagging shoulders? You smiled and straightened up real fast, didn't you?

A negative expression and poor posture reveal themselves in your voice. Smile! Your positive personality will be telegraphed naturally.

Sit down to make calls when you're looking your business best too. When you see that confident, polished professional smiling back at you from the mirror, the satellite will pick up your self-assured signals and beam them right to the hiring authority. You're in!

ACCENTUATE THE POSITIVE

Negativity is an insidious disease that attacks millions. A rapid heartbeat when talking with prospective employers is one major symptom.

If you make a telephone call and get a "no interest" response to your best interview delivery, don't hang up and immediately dial another prospect while you're experiencing the "No" woes. Maxwell Maltz noted in *Psycho-Cybernetics* that "A human being always acts and feels and performs in accordance with what he imagines to be true about himself and his environment. This is a basic and fundamental law of mind. It is the way we are built."[5]

This is the scientific explanation behind the need to "think positively." Each time you pick up the telephone, it's a new beginning—a chance for something better. You have to *think* you're a winner to *be* a winner. If you contract rejection shock, each phone call will become a self-fulfilling prophecy— rejection. If necessary, just keep reminding yourself that there are 100 million jobs out there, and you only need one of them. The right one, of course.

JUST FOLLOW THE FOLLOW-UP SCRIPT

You've already had practice making the deep-breath phone call. If you've been following my techniques throughout your job hunt, that first call was instrumental in getting you into your first interview. Now you're ready to go the distance. The follow-up phone call will create that opportunity for you.

Although I have emphasized that you are selling your skills and abilities to the highest bidder, one rule of the sale does *not* apply here. Don't "ask for the job."

It always surprises sales professionals when I give this advice, but I do it because I want to save you from looking like you're on your hands and knees. That's the wrong position to be in to interview properly.

The correct position is sitting erect and considering several offers. Instead of asking for the job, your pressure point is an *answer*, because you have "waited as long as you can," have "some decisions to make," and so on. Your firm but gentle tone will convey that message even though your words don't.

Sit comfortably at your desk, back straight, confident. Take a deep breath, exhale slowly, and make the call that will get you hired.

From *The Perfect Job Reference*, here's an example of how to make your telephone play:

Interviewer: Ed Wagner.

You: Hello, Mr. Wagner. (Note: Use "Miss" or "Mrs." only if you know the interviewer does so.) This is Donna Boardman.

Interviewer: Hello. I got your follow-up letter just a couple of days ago. No decision has been made yet, but I assure you that you're still being considered for the position.

You: That's good news. As I said in my letter, I'm very interested. I know I would be a good fit for the job. However, I'm in a difficult situation. I've been asked for a decision on another offer and I've delayed as

long as I can. I'd really rather work for Allied Equipment. Can you tell me when exactly I should hear
from you?

Interviewer: I understand. Let me see what I can do. I
can tell you you're one of two remaining candidates. I
have a meeting with the director at 3:00 to go over
this. I'll push for a decision.

You: Great! I really appreciate it. Shall I call you at 4:00?

Interviewer: Better make it 4:30.

You: I'll talk to you then. Thank you.

Interviewer: Goodbye.

You: Goodbye.

Now *that's* a follow-up phone call charged with positive
energy. It's almost certain that you will be the decision the
decision-maker makes.

Even if you and the other candidates are *equally* qualified, you're the one who will be calling back for the news,
and most hiring officials avoid giving bad news more than
job seekers avoid receiving it. You've given yourself a for-
midable edge. And your competitors won't even know
why they lost the race.

While you're always at an advantage if you catch the
decision-maker in the midst of pondering his or her decision, you're still ahead even if you catch him or her off
guard. As I mentioned earlier, that's the way I got hired
for that legal assistant job.

Here's how your "close encounter of the hiring kind"
might go.

Decision-Maker: Oh, yes, Ms. Boardman. Let me see if I

remember correctly. You were the engineer with an MBA from, where was it, San Francisco State University?

You: No, that must have been *another* candidate. *My* MBA is from Stanford. I graduated with high honors two years ago from their Executive Management Program. I have 15 years' experience as a senior engineer for Standard Products Company.

Decision-Maker: Now I remember. Very impressive credentials.

You: (Your best line) I have the combination of education and experience to do the job you need done. I'd be surprised if you've run across *anyone* better prepared than I am.

Decision-Maker: No, that's true. But we have other things to consider.

You: Are you at liberty to discuss them?

Decision-Maker: Well, for example, we're concerned about bringing in someone from the outside. The department resulted from the merger of two others. There have been staff layoffs, and the job requires someone who can improve morale. An outsider may not be able to do that.

You: If you review my reference letters, you'll note that the people who have worked for me have spoken highly of my skills as a team builder. Maybe an outsider is just what you need for this touchy situation. Someone without a history at the company, with no preconceived ideas and hidden agendas. I think I'm that person.

Decision-Maker: That's an excellent point, and it probably just won you the game, Ms. Boardman. When did
you say you can start?[6]

Now maybe you won't get hired over the phone. The
higher the position you've targeted, the less likely that is. Play
this inning right, though, and you will get invited back for
more interviews.

THE WORST AND THE BEST

If you still find you can't battle the telephone butterflies, talk
yourself into phoning. Ask yourself:

"What's the worst that can happen?"

The worst that can happen is that your contact will say
something like, "Gee—I've been meaning to let you know that
we won't be able to use you at this time."

You would have received this response whether you
phoned or not; and isn't it lucky that you have your contact
handy when it happens! It gives you the perfect opportunity to
express both your regrets and your hope that you may work together in the future. And while you're on the subject, and the
phone, you can turn your ex-target into a mentor, thus giving
strokes and getting feedback and advice.

After you hang up (and calm down), write a note along
those same lines to the interviewer, with your thanks.

And that's the worst that can happen. No worse than if
you didn't call, and maybe better.

The next worst that can happen? Simple: You simply
don't get through to your target. So you're even.

And the best that can happen?

Right then and there, by phone, you set up your follow-up interview.

Chapter

7

Conducting Each Follow-Up Interview Perfectly

Replay to Win

Your inventory beefed up your resume. Your resume won you the first interview. The impression you made there, backed by the power of your references and the skills of your follow-up letters and calls, have won a second interview.

You're in extra innings now, and the game is close. You may even be beginning to sweat. And sweat you should (ahead of time, please). Because even though it's true that the second interview is almost equated with getting the job, in this game "almost" doesn't count.

The "up" sides of second and subsequent interviews do count in your favor because:

- You can really go into them "up," with boosted confidence that you've been doing something right enough to get you there.

- You can prepare even more fully for them. Not only do you have your research notes to draw on, you've also learned a lot from your previous meeting and all your follow-up contacts.

You can't assume that the second interview will be only a replay of the first. In fact, it's sure to be different, though your basic approach stays the same.

THE SAME . . .

You'll put into play at your subsequent encounters all of the techniques that you employed (obviously with success) during your first interview.

Align with the Interviewer

Will Rogers said, "I never met a man I didn't like." Jeff Allen says, "Neither did I. That's why I never saw a job I couldn't get."

An employment interview is a place to be *liked.* Unless you're likeable, you won't be hireable.

On my first day as an employment interviewer, I was warned to guard against any applicant's "halo effect." Twenty-five years later, I still can't tell you how to do this. The halo effect is a phenomenon that occurs when the interviewer identifies with the applicant. Once it happens, the applicant can't do or say anything wrong. The halo effect gives a job seeker the psychological advantage that will zap any interviewer into submission within seconds.

Use the "Tie-Down" Technique to Move the Interview Along

Listening and *questioning* properly is the way to win the interview. For the first few minutes of the interview, you're observing and determining how to proceed. You've been asked impossible questions and have delivered inspirational answers.

Now you must ask questions—*carefully.* In the recruiter's rulebook *Closing on Objections,* Paul Hawkinson wrote:

Constant questioning can be grating, and if overused, can work against you. No one wants to feel that they are on the receiving end of the prosecutor's interrogatory and questions must be used sparingly to be really effective. But they are necessary because *selling is the art of asking the right questions* to get to the minor yes's that allow you to lead . . . to the major decision and major yes. The final placement is nothing more than the sum total of all your yes's throughout the process. Your job, then, is to nurse the process along [emphasis added].[1]

Moving the process along is done through the use of "tie-down" phrases in questions designed to elicit an affirmative response. The most common ones are:

- Aren't I/you/we/they?
- Can't I/he/she/you/we/they/it?
- Doesn't he/she/it?
- Don't I/you/we/they?
- Don't you agree?
- Hasn't he/she/it?
- Haven't I/you/we/they?
- Isn't he/she/it?
- Isn't that right?
- Shouldn't I/he/she/you/we/they it?
- Wasn't I/he/she/it?
- Weren't you/we/they?
- Won't I/he/she/you/we/they/it?
- Wouldn't I/he/she/you/we/they/it?

There are four kinds of tie-downs, and you should vary your dialogue with them so you won't appear obvious or over-bearing. With each agreement you obtain from the interviewer, you have scored one more "minor yes" leading up to that "major yes"—the offer.

The Standard Tie-Down

These are used at the end of a question:

"My qualifications appear to fit the position you have open, don't they?"

"Diversified Investments really has a lot to offer someone with my experience, doesn't it?"

"It looks like we'll be able to eliminate the problem, don't you agree?"

The Inverted Tie-Down

These are used at the beginning of a question:

"Isn't it an excellent position for someone with my background?"

"Don't you think we'll be working together well?"

"Wouldn't you like to see how I can be of assistance?"

The Internal Tie-Down

These are used in the middle of a compound question:

"Since the entire data processing staff agrees, shouldn't we discuss when I can start work?"

"When the budget is approved, won't it expedite production to have someone who knows the project?"

"Now that we've had the opportunity to meet, wouldn't it be great to work together?"

The Tag-On Tie-Down

The final kind of tie-down is used after a statement of fact. A slight pause, then emphasis on the tie-down, improves its effect:

> "My experience will benefit Allied Products, won't it?"
>
> "You've really spent a lot of time and money to get the right person, haven't you?"
>
> "This problem can be corrected easily, can't it?"

The best way to learn tie-down questioning techniques is the same way you rehearse your script for the interview. You write down all the tie-down lines you can use during the interview, then read them into a tape recorder and play them back once or twice a day—every day—to implant them into your subconscious. They'll pop out automatically when you need them.

After about a week of this exercise, the tie-down technique will come naturally to you. You can begin your dialogue with a general question, such as:

> "National Manufacturing leads the market with this product, doesn't it?"

Then hone in with questions such as:

> "Wouldn't it be interesting to work for a supervisor like that?"

And, finally:

> "Shouldn't I give notice?"

Remember: Overuse of questions will make you sound like you're auditioning for a game show rather than taking a screen test. Use them sparingly for best results.

Find an Area of Agreement, and Lead Slowly and Carefully to the Offer

When you hear a positive comment such as "This is the kind of experience we need," lean forward slightly in your seat, smile, and try one of these:

"My background fits this position very well."

"We have a good match here."

"This looks like a long-term situation."

"I'm excited about the position."

These statements gently "close" the interview with class. The interviewers don't know and don't care whether you're using closing techniques. That's because they're dealing with a qualified candidate who knows how to play *their* game.

. . . BUT WITH BIG DIFFERENCES

All well and good. But the second interview *isn't* the same as the first one. The heat is on, and the rematch is different in more than degree:

You'll likely be talking with someone different.

At the very least, some new players will join the field. You'll be dealing with some of the first string this time.

Power Interview Techniques

The following techniques, which worked so well during your initial interview, carry even more power when put into play with the top brass.

Attempt to Sit Next to the Interviewer

If there's a couch in the office, stand there until you are asked to be seated, since that's the best place for your interview. You create an atmosphere of "you and me against the job opening" rather than "you against me."

The opportunity will probably arise to sit on your favored side (your right—the interviewer's left—if you're right-handed, etc.). This is because over 95 percent of the time there are two chairs facing the interviewer. That favored side is psychologically your *power* side. Sitting there will cause you to interview more confidently.

Look for an opportunity to walk around to the interviewer's side during the interview so you can look at some report, chart, or project "together."

Remember the lessons of the four personality types. The director and thinker personalities need more space between themselves and you. They're not comfortable with air space invasions and could react negatively if you move in too close.

"Mirror" the Interviewer's Body Language, Facial Expressions, Eye Movement, Rate of Speech, Tone of Voice, and Rate of Breathing

Note that I said "mirror," not "mimic." This is a subtle art, and you'll need practice to get it right. The results will amaze and amuse you, however. This subtle form of imitation is a proven way to establish rapport. Just be careful to *align*, not *offend*. With practice, mirroring will become natural for you. It's a basic form of physical agreement.

Use "Insider" Language

The company buzzwords and insider language I told you to leave off your resume in *Jeff Allen's Best: The Resume* should be used during a follow-up interview. Every group has its own verbal shorthand that its members use constantly.

The primary use of insider language in pacing is to lock in the alignment with the interviewer. It's a linguistic password that gets you into the interviewer's thinking process and allows you to lead. It also signifies that you are compatible with the corporate culture.

"Company" buzzwords should be heard and noted in your job search research and phonework. Understand and use them correctly.

Because of the presence of new participants, in part,

the tone of the conversation will be different.

On the one hand, you can expect to be welcomed as a colleague, or at least a peer. On the other hand, you'll sense a closer examination, not simply of your qualifications, but of your character and personality. If your prospective employers didn't feel you could do the job, they wouldn't have invited you back. Now, they're more interested in determining what kind of person you'll be to work with.

Therefore, the substance of the talk will be different as well.

Here's how to deal successfully with the differences.

Scout the Field

When you've been invited back for a follow-up interview, don't just wonder what the game plan is. Take the direct approach. Call your original interviewer, and after expressing your appreciation for the time he or she spent with you then, lead into the discussion with a comment something like: "From what I understand, it looks like I'll really be able to assist

_____. Is there anything I should know before we meet?"

Then listen and take notes. Interviewers will be delighted to give you their impressions. Often they are extremely incisive since they have access to the personnel files. Before you conclude the conversation, ask the interviewer if he or she thinks the supervisor would mind a direct call. Interpret "No, I don't" as a suggestion that you do so.

Then call the supervisor. After saying that the interviewer suggested you call, and asking whether he or she has a few minutes, state: "I'm looking forward to meeting you (again) on _____, at _____. Before we get together, I wonder if there's anything you'd like me to bring?"

The supervisor will not be able to think that fast. In the remote event that he or she asks for something, evaluate whether it can affect your chances adversely. If so, say something like: "I'll check to see whether I have it. If not, I'll bring what I can."

This is more than just an excuse to confirm the interview. It is a chance to hear where the supervisor's thinking is going with regard to hiring you. A little industrial espionage goes a long way—and you don't have far to go.

Generally, the second interview is more *directed*. It takes one of two paths, and you should prepare for both.

The first is

The "Who Are You?" Interview

This is similar to the first interview, with the interviewer asking you a lot of questions and you delivering perfectly timed responses. The difference is that you've now developed a clearer profile of your interviewer and the target job (with a little help from your friends) and know what drives the audience wild. Then there's

The "What Can You Do For Us?" Interview

This interview tends to be informational, rather than personal. Review your scripts and your notes to rehearse the buzzwords, inside information, and technical data. Be prepared to demonstrate exactly how your background, experience, and skills enable you to do the target job. It's a more objective approach, and you can be fully prepared.

Finally, there's

The Interrogation Interview

If you haven't already experienced the interrogation interview, you *may* have the opportunity at your rematch. And it *is* an opportunity. Hope it happens!

Why?

As I explained in *How to Turn an Interview into a Job*:

Gaining confidence in this situation is just a matter of practicing answering difficult questions in front of a mirror, with a tape recorder running. The typical interrogatories below are some, but certainly not all, the questions you may be asked. The answers demonstrate the technique, but must be honest for you. If you decide to rehearse your own answers, be sure that you come out of each one neutralizing the sting of the question. Of course you should adapt the actual wording to your own way of speaking.

Remember, you want to sound as though you were thinking of the question yourself. Answer in a sincere, direct manner, and move through the volley as quickly as courtesy will allow, so you can transform the interrogation interview into the irresistible interview.

Here are the questions and answers you can expect—and turn to your advantage—in an interrogation interview.[2]

1. Why are you planning to leave your present job?

I'd like to have responsibility and learn more about the area of _____. The potential in my present position is no longer high because of the (a) emphasis of the company on other areas, (b) size of the company, (c) limited product line.

2. How high do you think you can move in our company?

Eventually, I'd like to work my way up to being _____. Of course this will depend on several factors. I think the environment in _____ is conducive to the development of its employees. Your _____, _____, and _____ are all excellent. I'm interested in contributing to its goals and know my efforts will be recognized.

3. What is your preference in a new position?

I've found that as with almost anything else, you get back what you give. Every job has its challenges. The satisfaction of doing a good job is often its own reward too.

4. What are your career goals?

I'm looking for a company where I can contribute to its goals. _____ has a reputation for rewards according to performance. Therefore, my goals are to work toward becoming a _____. I want to learn as much as I can, so that as the possibility to move arises, I'll be ready.

5. Why should we offer you a job?

I've talked with a number of your employees and know _____ by reputation. There seems to be a perfect fit, and my employment would likely become a long-term relationship.

6. What can you do for us that another person won't be able to do?

My references are the best people to answer this question. I know they'd agree that I do my best whenever I'm working. Unfortunately, some people consider work to be a place for excuses rather than excellence.

7. Do you like working for someone else?

Yes. There is a saying, "Work is not only the way to make a living, it's the way to make a life." It's true. I'm a work-oriented person, and really enjoy being a

_____.

8. What kind of salary are you worth?

This should be according to my contribution to _____. While I expect more favorable compensation to make a move, I know you will be fair.

9. What were the three major accomplishments in your prior job?

_____

_____

_____

10. What were the three major accomplishments in your career?

_____

_____

_____

11. Do you work well with deadlines?

Yes. I work well when a deadline exists. I recall in my last job, _____. In our competitive business environment, deadlines are a way of life.

12. What types of people do you like?

My acquaintances are varied, but all have two things in common: dependability and personal integrity. Above all, I like people who can be trusted. Trust counts for a lot.

13. What types of people do you dislike?

Those who are even marginally dishonest—even with themselves. Candidly discussing differences with the other person can go a long way toward resolving them. As long as the integrity's there, almost anything can be resolved.

14. Why didn't you do better in school?

I guess I was involved with outside interests and my family responsibilities. I always was well liked by my teachers and classmates. I won awards for _____ _____ and was recognized for _____.

15. Why did you move from one job to another so often?

There were a number of factors beyond my control. At _____, it was a matter of no opportunity for advancement. My supervisor was an excellent instructor, and I assumed his duties regularly. However, there was just no room for advancement. At _____, the division was purchased by _____, and the plant was closed. I accepted a position with

_____, and planned to remain there on a long-term basis. But _____ recruited me away with a 17 percent increase and exciting prospects for career advancement in a growing environment. But the sales of _____ dropped due to competition from imports, and I could not advance there.

16. What is your main strength?

It is probably my desire to honor my commitments. I take great pride in delivering on my promises—on the job and in my personal life. I'm also able to get along with people, regardless of their backgrounds or personalities.

17. What is your main weakness?

Sometimes I tend to be preoccupied with doing my job. Then again, that might be considered a strength too.

18. What gets you angry?

Very little. I am generally very patient with others. People who intentionally do not perform their jobs properly get me annoyed. An employer and a customer deserve the most for their money, and they get it when those who make a product make it as well as they can.

19. How long would it take you to contribute to our organization?

It should be soon after I start. I know my job, learn fast, and require a lot from myself.

20. How long would you stay with us?

As far as I'm concerned, this should be for a long time. The "corporate culture" here fits my personality, and the relationship should be a successful one.

21. Would you be ready to travel?

Absolutely. Traveling is essential to conducting business. I'm used to it and adapt readily to new places and faces.

22. Would you be ready to relocate?

If you are: Yes. There are very few places I find unpleasant. Every city has its better areas. Really, the only differences are the weather and the accents of the people there. We can always return here for a vacation.

If you are not: Only if the opportunity is truly outstanding, since it would be unsettling to my family. But I don't rule it out. If there's a potential for making a bigger contribution, I'm interested.

23. What do you expect to be doing in five years?

This depends not only on my accomplishments, but also on the opportunities within the organization. However, I hope to be in a position of responsibility in the _____ area.

24. What is your opinion of your last boss?

I like my manager, and like the chance he gave me to contribute. My desire to leave relates more to being unable to use my potential.

25. Why didn't you obtain a job before this?

I've rejected several offers. However, this opportunity appears exceptional.

26. What parts of your previous jobs did you like?

_____

_____

_____

27. What parts of your previous jobs did you dislike?

_____

_____

_____

28. Could you relate a few times when your work was criticized?

I really can't recall any major criticisms. If anything, I've been complimented on it regularly. . . . Oh yes, once someone made a comment about _____, but _____.

29. What books have you read lately?

[Pick a popular nonfiction book to mention.]

30. What movies have you seen lately?

[Pick a popular general-interest movie in the theater or on television to mention.]

31. What do you like most about this position?

The contribution I can make by _____. I like everything about it.

32. What do you like least about this position?

There doesn't appear to be anything that I dislike.

33. Don't you think you would be happier in a different organization?

No. I've researched this company and the job thoroughly. The overall environment and the position you are offering make it particularly attractive.

34. Shouldn't you be earning more money?

I'm earning more than most people in my field. Job satisfaction and potential for advancement are important also.

35. Won't you try to take over your boss's job?

No. However, part of my job is to help my supervisor in [his/her] career. I should also be ready to take over for [him/her]. In that sense I'll be after [his/her] job.

36. In what ways are you creative?

Every job can be done better. In my last job, I _____ .

37. In what ways are you analytical?

Analyzing properly is an important part of being a good _____ . In my last job, I _____ .

38. What is your personality like?

Balanced. There are two sides to every issue, and I usually find that more can be done when people work together. I try to view things as "you and me against the *problem*," rather than "*you* against *me*."

39. What do you enjoy doing in your spare time?

I'm an avid reader in the _____ area. It helps me be a more productive _____, and I can bring new concepts to the job. I also spend time doing _____, since I enjoy my work even when I'm not technically working. I really enjoy being with my family too.

40. How do you get along with your family?

Very well. My family is an important part of my life. This makes it much more fulfilling.

41. What is your subordinates' opinion of you?

They respect me and know we have a job to do together. I try to praise them for their achievements and have taught them to assume my duties when I'm not there.

42. Do you delegate frequently?

Yes. This is an important management technique. Your subordinates must be trained to assume the duties delegated. In my last job, I _____.

43. What attributes do you desire in those you hire?

I look for a desire to work and to learn more. The ability to work with others is also critical, because few jobs can be done best alone.

44. What reasons caused you to fire people?

Generally poor work performance. I have high expectations, and not everyone is dedicated to doing his best at all times.

45. What kinds of jobs are you considering?

[Mention the elements of the job the company is offering.]

46. What employers are you considering?

I'd prefer not to mention them, because they want to hire me. They are companies a lot like this one, though.

47. What size employer do you want to work for?

It doesn't matter. The size of this company seems to be the best size because _____.

48. Tell us about yourself.

I was born and raised in _____, and was educated at _____ with a major in _____. I was first hired by _____, and have held increasingly responsible positions in the _____ field.

49. May we contact your last employer?

Yes, once we get together. For obvious reasons, I'd appreciate no communication until we've agreed on my employment. I'll probably receive a counteroffer and would prefer to be the first to tell my employer. Management would appreciate that.

50. May we contact your references?

Yes, once mutual interest has been established. I listed successful people who know my personal and professional qualifications thoroughly, but I don't want to impose on them. If you let me know when you need the contact information, I'll provide it.[3]

Special situations can arise when you've progressed beyond the initial job-hunting rounds. By and large, they're unavoidable, but you can predict, prepare, and control them too.

TABLE TALK

In job hunting, there's no such thing as a free meal. In fact, if a target invites you to breakfast, lunch, or dinner and you approach it as though it were a friendly social occasion, it could well be the most expensive meal that ever caused you indigestion.

It's because mealtime encounters are so tricky that I've strongly advised you to avoid them whenever possible. But it's also because they're such a challenge that many prospective employers, especially when higher level jobs are on the line, insist on them.

When the interviewer insists on a mealtime "chat," you especially need to go into your alert mode.

Social psychologists closely study the mealtime behavior of families and other small groups because it is so revealing of the interplay of power and influence.

In the mealtime setting, people quite literally put their characters on the table. Your eating (and drinking) habits tell a lot about you, without your even being aware of it. At least, that's what your prospect expects. You have so much to think about, it's assumed, that you'll demonstrate by your unconscious actions not only whether you know how to "behave" in a social situation, but also such attributes of character and personality as consideration for others or an interest in taking good care of yourself.

So the first piece of advice for mealtime interviews is: Be aware! You are the main course on this menu, so act accordingly.

Mind Your Manners

If you have any doubts about your skill in handling several forks, read a book or take a course. Or just remember Emily Post—in all matters take a cue from your host. This is a refinement of the alignment technique. Do your best to imitate, within reason, your host's manners and choices.

Sit Strategically

You may not have a choice in where to sit, but try to maneuver yourself into a *power* sitting position in relation to your interviewer: close, but where you can see his or her face. If there are just two of you, and the table is small, sitting opposite is fine. Otherwise, if the table is large or if you are eating with more than one host, try to sit just to the left of the most important interviewer. (That is, if you are right-handed. If you are left-handed, sit to the interviewer's right so that you don't bump him or her while using your knife and fork.)

Eat Sensibly

Don't select the most expensive item on the menu—this indicates arrogance. Don't select the cheapest, either—this can be insulting, and it may lead your host to suspect you have a low level of self-esteem.

Choose healthy foods, but don't be too prim. In this age of diet consciousness, selections that are high in fats or cholesterol may worry a potential employer. But if you indulge only in tofu and greens, you may get tagged as a "food freak."

If possible, follow the lead of your host. But select items that are not difficult to handle or to chew. You have enough to think about without having to debone a Cornish hen. And you'll need to talk easily, so better an omelet than a salad.

Hide Your Habits

If you're a smoker, don't smoke unless your host picks a table in the smoking section of the restaurant and lights up first. Even then, smoke sparingly if at all. (If you're not a smoker, don't pick this occasion to discuss the dangers of second-hand smoke.)

If you're a drinker, don't drink. Again, follow the cues of your host—to an extent. Order a nonalcoholic (or at most a very light) before-meal drink, and if there's wine with a meal, don't finish your glass. Even if your hosts are drinking heartily, don't join in. Awareness of "addictions" is so great these days that it doesn't take much to cause alarm. Besides, you want your head clear and your tongue unfuzzy.

And if you're not a drinker, don't drink now! If you're unaccustomed to drinking at midday, there's nothing like the alcohol in even a wine spritzer to loosen your tongue inappropriately. If dinner time brings cocktails and wine, you have to assume that your hosts are used to it. If you're not, you could be in trouble. You needn't refuse the wine, just don't drink it. Water's wet enough.

The same interview etiquette applies to other social situations as well. You may be invited to get together with a few prospective colleagues. This is a good sign, probably. But it's also a test, and whether it shows or not, you are the "guest of honor," under constant observation. If your spouse is invited, it's even a better sign. But under doubly close scrutiny, both of you have to mind your manners.

HOW FAR WILL YOU GO?

If you're invited back for interviews or you're invited to go to the company headquarters in another city, great! This means for sure that you're on the "short list" for the job. Since it costs you nothing, you might as well go. And you should go, to demonstrate your enthusiasm for the job.

Beware of seeming *too* eager, though. Make it clear that you are an important person and have important things to do (whether you do or not), so that you must have some say in the scheduling of this venture. It's okay, too, to clarify in advance the procedures for having your expenses paid: Will you make the arrangements, and be reimbursed? Will they purchase the tickets? How will you receive them? And so forth. Just be businesslike about this.

And remember, once you're there, you're on *their* turf. Everything advised about mealtime interviews goes triple for your behavior during the days and nights your prospects have for "prospecting" you.

If you're invited out of town with *no* mention made of having your expenses paid, you can assume that you're expected to pay your own way. Points to consider in this circumstance:

- How much do you want the job?
- What do your information and intuition tell you about your chances for the job?
- Can you afford the time and expense of the trip?

If you really want the job and think you have a pretty good shot at it, you'll be able to figure out how to manage the trip. If money is tight, try to do it in one day, to avoid a hotel bill. Or plan it far enough in advance to get a less expensive plane fare. Depending on your circumstances and the current tax laws, you may at least be able to deduct the trip as a business expense. Then make your plans as close to the interviewer's convenience as possible, while letting it show that you are making—and are willing to make—a sacrifice for this employer.

If you're *not* willing to make this kind of sacrifice, don't. The job may not be worth it to you; you'll have other chances. Or you may sense that the real interest in you as an employee is really not that high. Or you simply may not be able to afford the trip.

But don't *tell* them any of that. Instead, say: "I'm sorry to have to miss the opportunity of talking with _____, but I'm afraid it really wouldn't be convenient for me to make the trip right now. My schedule is just too full."

This kind of "Thanks, but no thanks" can work to your advantage. Your interviewers may well respond by trying to make things more convenient for you. They may tell you that Mr. or Ms. Big will be coming to town after all, so why not come by for a talk? They may even offer to pay your way out of town.

If the company makes *any* move to encourage you to participate in this out-of-the-way interview, go out of your way to say "Yes." This means that they really are interested in you, and that's a good place for you to be.

If no such moves are made, that's okay too. It shows that the company is not such a hot prospect, and you're free to focus your energies elsewhere.

THE FINAL SCORE

After your follow-up interview or interviews, you can review, rerun, and rehash as you did after your first encounter. The only difference now is that you have almost nothing to do but wait. Almost.

However you score yourself, you've done the best you could, and it's done. Almost.

Again, *almost* isn't *all.*

The best way to play the waiting game is *not to wait.* Keep moving. No matter how confident you feel about getting that target job, turn your attention to other prospects, other contacts. This will keep you too busy to brood, and it will also keep you in play, just in case the answer is "No."

But almost harder to endure than a "No" answer is *no* answer. How long do you wait for a response? How do you initiate a response?

You can probably pick up the answers to these questions during the interview itself. For example, your interviewer may mention a time frame directly: "We're hoping to fill this position within the month." Or indirectly: "The new sales season begins next month. It's going to be a tough one."

You may be able to sense how urgent or relaxed the deadline is. Or you can ask: "Can you give me an idea of when you're planning to come to a decision on this position?" After all, you have important plans of your own to make—or at least you can leave them with that impression.

When you mail your brief thank-you note after the interview, you can close with something like, "I'll call your office next week to see if there's anything else you need from me."

In any event, if a response doesn't come immediately, you need to allow a little longer than you did for the simple rescheduling of an interview. Put a memo in your calendar for two weeks hence, and if you haven't heard by then, call.

Once you get your answer, if you've perfected your follow-ups and all that led up to them, it's likely to be a "Yes."

And where you go from "Yes" determines whether the job you win is a winning job.

Chapter

8

Follow Up After the Job Offer

Realize Your Goal, Then Renegotiate It

"**Y**ou're hired." Every job seeker's dream words. Or, more likely: "We're happy to say that we can offer you a job with our organization."

No matter how it's phrased—no matter how happy you are to hear it—you don't *have* to accept.

In fact, you shouldn't.

What?

Isn't this book about winning the job? If the umpire says "safe," you're in, right? And didn't those words just win you the job?

If you've come this far, yes; you've won *a* job. But you may not have won *the* job that makes you a winner.

Most career books end at the "you're hired" point. But this one is about follow-up. Now it's time for follow-*through*.

COOL DOWN

What's fun about this part of the game is that, if you do it right, both you and your new employers will win. They get the employee they want; you get the job you want.

You've plotted your strategy successfully so far, and you've played through to the ninth inning. But the last pitch hasn't been thrown yet. Don't let them throw you a curve. Be ready to make *your* final pitch a winning one.

You *will* have some advance warning that an offer is on the way. You'll have heard comments such as:

"When you join the team . . ."

"Your ideas will definitely help solve . . ."

"The sooner you can begin . . ."

But when you actually hear the job offer, you may react internally with surprise and excitement.

It's time to take a deep breath, literally and metaphorically. Cool down. Evaluate your position. If you must carry on a conversation while you do that, use noncommittal phrases such as:

"Well, that's very nice to hear." or

"I certainly appreciate the offer."

Flip your notebook to the page where you've listed your job wants and needs. That checklist should include:

- Salary: 10 to 20 percent more than your previous salary, unless outweighed by:
- Bonus
- Benefits
- Expense accounts
- Company car
- Relocation
- Vacation time

SPEAK UP—AND LISTEN HARD

All of the topics that have been taboo in previous interviews are on the table now.

What do you want? More!

Here's how to get it.

We've already noted that you should not disclose *any* salary on your resume. You should also avoid any discussion of it during the interview. Interrogation interviewers may try to corner you, but the best answer is always that your salary should be relative to your contribution to the employer.

If you follow this advice long enough, you may actually find interviewers who *forget* to confirm the salary before extending the offer! This is not unusual, because your salary is one of the last things that concerns an interviewer. Interviewers and supervisors can often increase an offer if they really want you too.

Another reason to defer salary discussions in larger companies is to slide by the initial interviewers to the person you will be working for. This is because personnel "manglers" are usually responsible for employment *and* wage and "slavery" administration. They have a vested interest in their own empire, and a love of procedures.

What do *you* want? More!

And you deserve it.

You may need to convince yourself of that, especially if you've been through unrewarding compensation conversations in the past.

In fact, in order to maximize your effectiveness at negotiating with the interviewer, you should reflect on the salary soap operas that have victimized you in the past. If necessary, write down their scripts and relive them just long enough to understand that they really had nothing to do with your performance at all, only the way it was *perceived*.

How do I know? Here's the secret:

The better the job you did, the more you felt you were entitled to the raise, and the worse you felt when you didn't get it.

You'll take a completely opposite approach in negotiating a salary from the one you used in asking for a raise. This is because it's an arm's-length transaction, and you are just an unread book with a high-quality cover.

You may happen to know more about the salary offered than the interviewer knows about your wants. Fine. Keep it to yourself.

If you are fortunate enough to know the salary because it is in the interviewer's spiel, *don't react.* If you know through a telephone inquiry, advertisement, internal referral, placement service, or other source, acknowledge this, but again, *don't react.*

Until you hear an absolute number, you are considering the options. Of course, it would be "inappropriate" to discuss other offers—downright "unprofessional," in fact. This isn't just being professional or polite. It's being smart.

You are in a stronger position to discuss money if the employer has already committed himself by offering you the job.

Negotiating a salary is similar to negotiating a loan: The more you appear to need it, the less likely you are to receive it. Let the two precepts of the art of negotiating work for you:

1. **The one who does the most talking ends up giving away the store.**
2. **The less you sweat, the more you'll get.**

Contemplate. Let the interviewers negotiate . . . against themselves. The question of whether you should ever disclose your present salary is something that you will have to decide for yourself. Salary is easy to verify by requiring proof from you (check stubs, tax returns, etc.) or contacting your last or present employer (a customary ritual). Curiously enough, the higher the position, the less likely it is that anyone will check.

If you are prepared, the answer to a question about your salary can be creative. State the amount you will receive after your next review and your chances of receiving an increase.

Overtime possibilities should also be included. What about probable bonuses? Consider pay in lieu of vacation, if that is available, since your new employer probably will not be allowing a vacation for a year. Include the monetary value to you of any unusual perks—whether company car, housing allowance, or personal expense accounts—especially those not offered by the new employer.

I am *not* recommending falsifying any information. I *am* recommending being aware of the hidden amounts that really add up. Remember, these are worth nothing if you don't include them, and 120 percent or more if you do. (The amount of the actual salary, plus the percentage of the increase you receive.)

Is their salary offer too low? Just not in the ballpark? Not to worry. With your job-hunting skills, this isn't the only offer you'll get. But before you reject it (or accept it out of desperation), weigh the *non*salary aspects of the job.

Evaluating a job offer requires you to consider carefully some important factors. They include the usual—salary, benefits, and career potential—as well as others you might not have given much thought.

MONEY ISN'T EVERYTHING

What will the working environment be like? How will it differ from what you are used to? If relocation is involved, how will your family be affected? Peak performance on the new job will be aided by a supportive, organized personal life.

If you're out of work now, you may not feel you have the luxury of choosing. But you do. You owe it to yourself, your family, and your employer to find the best possible job from an infinite inventory.

- If accepting the offer would require relocation, learn exactly how much leeway you have in a starting date.

You don't want to start a new position under the pressure of a rushed move.

- Analyze the positions below and above the target job. If the title is "manager," but there is no one reporting to you, determine just how much authority and support you will have.

- If the position is new, find out how you will relate to other positions in the company. Some creative negotiating now will make the target job much easier.

NEVER ASSUME

You also need to be sure that the job they're offering is the one you've been going after.

Never assume. Instead, clarify. Check your notes again, and be prepared to discuss:

- Title.
- Authority.
- Staffing.
- Position within organization.
- Performance expectations.
- Travel demands.
- Advancement opportunities.

Begin by saying, "Now, as I understand it . . ." and proceed through the items on that checklist. As you cover each topic:

- Recap what's been said in interviews, *and*
- Describe what *you* expect (and want).

A candidate who knows the job description would say:

As I understand it, I will be the manager for new business development, reporting to the marketing director. My salary will be $70,000, with a bonus of $5,000 and future increases based on productivity. You provide full medical, dental, disability, and life coverage. I will have a staff of three, including a market researcher, a program analyst, and an administrator, as well as secretarial help. I'll need to travel less than 25 percent of the time. Since I'll have to relocate in order to take this job, you will reimburse me for all moving and interim living expenses.

If possible, get this offer in writing. Never fear; this step should be easy too. And it could stand you in very good stead at some later date. While your prospective employers are nodding their heads after you review the terrific offer you've just received, tie it down with: "Great. So I don't see why we shouldn't put all this in a note, do you? It will help me keep all this in mind while I'm making my final decision."

Your prospective employer should have no problem with putting it in writing.

BELIEVE IT? OR NOT?

At these final stages, your job hunt is, for sure, no longer a game. Your life—a good part of it, anyway—depends on what you come away with. So come away from these end-game conversations with more than words.

Now, while you're engaged in serious negotiations and clarifications, is also a time to keep your sensors extra alert and your intuition active. A job is much more than work and an office. How do you *feel* about the people who are offering this job? Can you trust the offers they're making? Do you trust *them*? Do you feel comfortable in the environment? Do you feel comfortable with the people?

Draw on all you've learned and absorbed during the interviews and other contacts so far. If you have any reservations, make a mental note of them.

Even if all your reactions are positive, wait. Even if all the answers you're getting are the ones you want to hear, do *not* end the session with a handshake and an agreement. Instead, say, "Thank you. This sounds fine, but . . .

I want to talk with my family about it."

I have other offers I need to clarify."

I'd like to sleep on it."

STAY AWAKE

Then "sleep on it." But don't sleep any more than you have to. Instead, think about the offer, actively. Go back over your notes related to this organization. Refresh your memory about any doubts or questions you've had during the process. Weigh the job in writing. List the "pros" of this job and the "cons."

Talk about the offer. Discuss it with your spouse, your family, friends whose judgment you respect. Get feedback from your career mentors or others in your business whom you trust. (Your list of preference references should provide some good listeners.)

If you do have other offers or possibilities that intrigue you equally or more than this one, go to those prospects. Tell them that you've been offered a position elsewhere, but you'd prefer to work for *their* organization. They may make an even better offer. Or they may not. If they seem hesitant about a response, make it clear that you have a time limit. State your deadline.

If you have other potential opportunities, whether they're firm or not, make another comparison sheet. Note pro's and con's of Job A *versus* Job B *versus* Job C. Seeing that information on paper will help clarify your decision-making process. It may tell you to say "Yes" to the offer at hand, or it may suggest that you wait a bit and push harder for potential offers.

You should also indeed "sleep on it." You can do that actively too. When you settle down for the night, tell yourself that you want to come to a clear decision. Review the pro's and con's in your mind before you go to sleep. Your unconscious will continue to consider the issue while you rest.

In the morning, or soon, you will be able to:

ACCEPT WITH ASSURANCE

After evaluating the new job and deciding that it's a good opportunity, demonstrate confidence in your decision. The way you accept will set the stage for future negotiations after you start work. Emphasize how much you're "looking forward" to the "new challenge." In fact, you're "anticipating" the "opportunity" to "contribute."

If you have fully employed the job-seeking techniques I've been recommending, though, you should feel as solid and positive about your decision as your acceptance sounds.

Of course, you can *really* accept a job offer with absolute assurance if you have the details in writing. That's what the next chapter—covering the next-to-last "R"—is about.

Chapter

9

What Follows "Yes"—Employment Agreements

Require What You Want, Then Relax

Although this is Chapter 9, it's where you can score a "perfect 10." I'll show you how to negotiate a formal employment agreement. I'll also explain how you can at least be sure that in accepting the job, you're also providing yourself with some job security and protection against wrongful termination.

Employment agreements, or their equivalents, can ensure that your job is as close to perfect as possible in an imperfect world. These agreements *are* like insurance policies. They can keep you on the team and reward you for being on it.

Since your new employer wants you on the team, why not get what *you* want too? Although you should not expect to get an employment agreement unless your new position is in middle or upper management, employers today are surprisingly receptive to signing them. This agreeableness is not due to any particular openheartedness or openhandedness on the part of employers. Rather, in a legislative and judicial environment of enhanced employee-protection laws and decisions, employers see the need for written agreements to protect *themselves*.

As I cautioned employers in *The Employee Termination Handbook*:

> [A] steamroller has started, fueled by an increasing number of court decisions holding employers accountable for their firings. Those decided or pending include such household names as American Airlines, AT&T, ARCO,

Atari, Avco, Bissell, Blue Cross/Blue Shield, Firestone, IBM, McGraw-Hill and NCR. In fact the list already reads like a *Who's Who in Corporate America*. Back pay, front pay, punitive and exemplary damages are the rule, often totaling hundreds of thousands of dollars. Over 75 percent of the awards are in favor of the former employees.[1]

In this climate, employment agreements are like prenuptial contracts. With those to limit divorce settlements, the wealthier spouse [= your employer] is sure to lose *some* assets as a result of a marital split, but is protected against being totally ruined by an angry ex-mate [= you].

In *Perks and Parachutes* John Tarrant notes:

Written contracts are being offered in ever-increasing numbers to American white-collar employees. And while the most highly publicized contracts are given to board chairmen and chief executives, countless thousands of people in the middle-management area are under contract today, or will be negotiating contracts soon. If you make $30,000 a year or more, before too long you are likely to be confronting questions like these:

Is a contract to my advantage?
What should it cover?
How long should it run?
What are the dangers?
Can I earn the performance bonus called for in my contract?
What happens if I want to break my contract?
How can I negotiate the best possible agreement?[2]

The agreements you sign with your new employer *are* contracts. Like all contracts, they define what each party *gets*; they also require that each party *give* something. Keep in mind that your employer wants to give as little—and get as much—as possible, and you see why you must proceed carefully through the negotiation process.

"YES, BUT . . ."

You begin negotiating by saying, in effect, "Yes, but . . . ."

"Yes, I'll accept your job offer."

"But, here's what you must give me in return."

Remember that they've already said they want you. All you have to do is leverage their need and desire into what *you* need and desire.

It's not hard. It only takes practice.

When you try to develop a satisfactory employment contract, there are four "Ps" to keep in mind:

- Person
- Proper timing
- Presentation
- Policy

I discussed these in another of my books, *Finding the Right Job at Midlife.* Here are the highlights of the four-P formula.

Person

The person whose job it is to interview you is probably the last one you should discuss an employment contract with. Remember, most employment interviewers are administrators. Administrators are charged with administering the policies of others. Therefore, anything out of the ordinary or the company routine will seem just plain wrong to them.

Be sure you are talking with a decision-maker when you discuss employment agreements. Some are capable of making recommendations, but most aren't. Talk with someone who has actual hiring *authority.*

Proper Timing

From what you have read in this book so far, you should realize that you are in a good position to negotiate. Once you are employed, however, this position reverses dramatically. From my experience, about 80 percent of all employment agreements are negotiated before a person reports to work. But they are rarely, if ever, negotiated during the first interview.

Generally speaking, if you are called back for a second interview, you will be made an offer 60 percent of the time. At this point, you will probably be a lot more confident, and it will be a lot easier to deal with your interviewer. If you are offered the job at this point, this is the time to discuss an employment contract.

Presentation

When you are looking for a job, you are selling the most important commodity you have—yourself. Therefore, your presentation must be first rate. In fact, our office is so sure that the presentation is critical that we guarantee to refund half the fee if it doesn't get the job offer. After 10 years and preparing literally hundreds of presentations, we have had to live up to our guarantee only about 15 times.

Once you are offered the job, everyone is going to be feeling good. You will because you're getting the job you want. The interviewer will be in a good mood because he or she will have done the job expected. Now, when everyone is feeling good, you should suggest that a short agreement be prepared outlining the terms.

Some interviewers may feel uncomfortable with this, but you can solve the problem by simply offering to prepare it yourself and to deliver it the next day. To make it go easily, just say, "It's simply a memorandum of understanding, and I'll do it for you."

The important point to remember at this point is that you must keep the meeting positive and upbeat. Be enthusiastic. Don't make it sound as though you were running to a lawyer to hogtie the company.

Policy

Once you and your interviewer agree and you're going to prepare your memorandum of agreement, head home and switch on your wordprocessor. You're going to whip out your memorandum of agreement. Don't, whatever you do, title it "Employment Contract." It really is, but there's no need to raise a red flag here. If you do, everything will grind to a halt. Don't give them the opportunity to consider another candidate.

Here's all you have to say in your memorandum of agreement;

In consideration of (name of employer) (EMPLOYER) hiring (first name) (last name) (EMPLOYEE), it is agreed as follows:

[Typical Paragraph]

A total amount of $_____ per _____ shall be paid by EMPLOYER to EMPLOYEE, less any customary and usual deductions for the performance of services in the initial position of _____. Said total amount shall be increased by at least _____ percent per year on or before the anniversary date of EMPLOYEE. Changes in title or responsibilities shall be at the sole discretion of the EMPLOYER.

When you type this and the paragraphs that follow, make sure they look sharp.

Note that this paragraph discusses an important issue—money. Leave the percentage blank. It's important to give the supervisor the opportunity to negotiate this figure. No one likes to be told how much more he or she is going to pay you. But, by putting the blank in for agreement, you have taken the initiative in getting the subject on the table.

[Typical Paragraph]

If EMPLOYER terminates the employment of EMPLOYEE after 90 days for any reason other than a specific violation of a written policy formerly acknowledged by EMPLOYEE, _____ times the current weekly gross amount shall be immediately paid to EMPLOYEE. Said amount includes pay in place of notice and severance pay, but excludes any personal leave, sick leave, holiday, vacation, or other pro rata termination pay in accordance with the policy of EMPLOYER.

As you did with the first paragraph, you'll have to insert the severance pay figure. Try to determine how much the company ordinarily pays by making a quick call to the personnel department. Needless to say, don't let them know that you are creating an employment agreement. When you have the number, double it. For reference, four weeks is usually the most a newly hired person can receive.

For reasons other than those inherent in equal opportunity laws, employment is usually terminable at will. It just doesn't make sense to try to force an employer to retain your services.

[Typical Paragraph]

EMPLOYEE acknowledges that the internal procedures, lists, records, forms, and other proprietary information developed or obtained by EMPLOYER while conducting business are confidential trade secrets and shall remain the sole property of EMPLOYER. Accordingly, EMPLOYEE shall not retain, duplicate, disclose, or make use of any of said proprietary information except as required by the specifications of employment.

Using this paragraph is a good way to emphasize your professional responsibility. It simply states that you are familiar with the local and state laws, and that you are an ethical person. Further, it will help you avoid liability for unfair competition if you leave the company. As you probably know, many employers get very nervous when such things as trade secrets are at stake.

Employers are particularly impressed when you include this paragraph. I've seen this paragraph help get the agreement signed in a good many cases.

[Typical Paragraph]

EMPLOYEE agrees to act in an attentive, ethical, and responsible manner, and to represent exclusively the EMPLOYER at all times with the utmost concern for its goals, interests, and image with its employees, customers, suppliers, and all others with whom they come in contact during the conduct of business.

This is known as the "best efforts" paragraph. Some form of the wording is found in most employment agreements. But from your perspective, it's best to include because it counterbalances some of the items you want.

[Typical Paragraph]

If it becomes necessary for EMPLOYEE or EMPLOYER to enforce or interpret the terms of this Agreement, matters will be resolved by binding arbitration under the auspices and in accordance with the rules of the American Arbitration Association. Any judgment on the decision rendered may be entered in any court of competent jurisdiction.

This is an especially important paragraph simply because the company hiring you can better afford to litigate a dispute in the court system than you. It's not unusual for employees to drop a valid claim or to wipe out their mid-life savings in prosecuting or defending a court case. Binding arbitration is a thoroughly professional and far less expensive way to resolve a dispute.

[Typical Paragraph]

Neither EMPLOYEE nor EMPLOYER shall disclose either the existence of this Agreement or any of its terms for the duration of said employment. If EMPLOYEE directly or indirectly causes such disclosure, EMPLOYER may immediately terminate the employment, as though a written policy formerly acknowledged by EMPLOYEE had been violated.

There is little danger of you not keeping this agreement confidential. In fact, it's one of the most powerful devices you have to get the agreement signed immediately. I discussed the reasons for this earlier in this chapter.

OTHER WAYS TO AGREE

Your employer's policy may prohibit negotiating employment agreements. Even without a formal written legal-looking contract, you have other ways to protect yourself and to delineate your job.

Exchange Letters

If you've received your job offer in writing, as I recommended in the previous chapter, you're halfway to a written agreement that is the equivalent of an employment agreement. All you have to do is seal the deal by responding to your written job offer in writing.

Send a letter to the person who wrote your job offer repeating the offer as stated and spelling out your understanding regarding these key items:

- Duties.
- Length of employment.

- Salary and other compensation.
- Benefits.
- Termination.
- Severance pay.

A sample is shown in Figure 9.1.

Read Their Fine Print

Most employers, except for some very small enterprises, have employee handbooks. Many large organizations—both private corporations and public and quasi-public institutions—also have detailed, written personnel policies. Establishing grades, or ranks, and levels within them, these handbooks usually define each position and its duties.

Any such written document serves as an agreement between you and your employer. If you cannot negotiate an individual agreement, at least ask to see this material before accepting a new position. It provides details about the job that a prospective superviser may gloss over. It also defines the rights and responsibilities that will influence the outcome of any future conflict you may have with your employer after the new job glow fades.

What I advised in *Surviving Corporate Downsizing* applies to new hires as well:

> Employee handbooks and personnel policy manuals are being upheld as *binding contracts*. Here are some excerpts from typical handbooks.
>
> > The management of Company X is committed to the career development of each of its employees. All promotions and transfers will be made considering the preferences of the individuals involved.

Figure 9.1 Sample Acceptance Letter

November 11, 19__

Ms. Margaret O. Blaine, Product Manager
Convenience Foods Division
American Foods Company
1667 Commonwealth Avenue
Boston, Massachusetts 02210

Dear Ms. Blaine:

I am happy to accept your offer of employment in the position of assistant product manager.

I understand that I will be responsible for the development, sales, and marketing of American's line of children's snack foods, supervising a staff of two and reporting to you.

The travel schedule—approximately one week out of every month—which you described to me is manageable, since I understand that I will have the use of a company car.

The initial salary of $45,000 that you offer is agreeable to me, especially with your assurance of a bonus and a salary review within six months.

As you suggested, I have read the American Foods employee handbook, and I am impressed by the company's policies regarding health insurance, vacation and sick days, and termination notice and severance-pay arrangements.

Since I have given notice at my current job, I will indeed be able to start at American immediately after Thanksgiving.

I look forward to seeing you then, and I am enthusiastically anticipating becoming a part of American Foods.

With thanks,

Angela P. Edwards

Whenever possible, we strive to promote from within, recognizing that the success of our team depends upon the growth of its members.

Company X has a history of steady progress that has made it a leader in the areas it serves. Therefore, you can expect to be rewarded commensurate with your effort.

You'll find inspirational words from sea to shining sea about treating employees "fairly," "equitably," "equally," "consistently," "impartially," and "evenhandedly." Courts and legislatures have been so inspired by these words that they've elevated them to an "implied covenant," a *promise* of continued employment. However, the employee must *rely* on the promise. That's implied too by accepting the job and working there.

Personnel policy manuals are usually far more specific with regard to proclamations and procedures for everything from phone usage to insurance. Here are a few gems:

Decisions regarding termination of management personnel should be made objectively by the supervisor with the concurrence of his immediate supervisor. Factors to be considered include performance of the employee, length of employment, and reason for the termination.

Severance pay shall be based upon length of service and amount of earnings of the employee. It shall be computed at not less than two weeks pay for every year worked, or fraction thereof.

Company X is committed to a firm policy of equal employment opportunity. Management shall hire, promote, and transfer employees without regard to race, religion, national origin, age, sex, marital status or other discriminatory criteria.

These aren't even *implied* promises. They're detailed *expressed policies.*[3]

Second Thoughts

If you're about to accept a job from an employer who has *no* written policies and will sign no written agreement, you'd 'be wise to rethink your "Yes." Beware especially of any oral offer that sounds too good to be true, made by someone who seems too friendly to be real. The odds are such propositions turn out to be neither "true" nor "real." Follow up instead on an offer that may sound less exciting, but feels more solid.

Future conflicts shouldn't be a major cause of worry right now, though, particularly if you adhere to the advice and suggestions you've read here. Even if you do encounter imperfections down the pike, be assured that you do have a variety of legal protections and professionals to help you invoke them.

RELAX

For now, why not turn to the tenth "R" and relax? Enjoy the new-job glow. You've earned it. But you still need to turn your attention to a couple more "Rs."

Resign with Refinement

Don't burn any bridges. It takes forever to rebuild them, even if you don't get lost looking. Give proper notice, help in the hiring of your replacement, and train him or her if you can.

You never know when you'll meet up with these coworkers and supervisors again. You may need them. Remember your networking lessons; keep in touch.

Get a Reference Letter

As I noted in *The Perfect Job Reference*:

> The time to get a reference letter from a supervisor is *before* your coworkers cut your cake. This letter will come in handy in the future if your supervisor runs away from home, goes crazy, dies, or tries to block your career path.[4]

Before you ask for a reference letter, review your accomplishments and results in the position you are leaving, and draft a sample letter. Chances are your supervisor will sign with a sigh (of relief—because he or she won't have to prepare one).

Before you actually start the new job, take some time off; but make productive use of it. Go through all your recent job-seeking notes, record sheets, and files. Sort them out. Store them away in an organized fashion. The time may come when you're ready to search for an even more "perfect" job. If and when that happens, you won't have to start from scratch.

Last, but assuredly not least, tie up some vitally important personal loose ends. Contact everyone with whom you've had significant contact during this job hunt. Written contact is best.

Write first to any employer who may still be considering you as a candidate. Then write to any interviewers at organizations that particularly interested you. Both of these groups represent potential employers at some future date. Thank them again, graciously, for their time and consideration. Let them know that you have accepted employment elsewhere, but don't slam any doors. Instead, express hope that an opportunity may arise in the future for working with them. Leave them with a positive impression of you. That impression may open new doors someday.

Finally, be sure to contact (send a gift, if appropriate) anyone who provided a reference for you, who was ready to provide a reference, or who helped you in any other way to win the job you are about to enjoy. These people went out of their way for you. Make sure they feel it was worth doing. Who knows? You may ask them to do it again someday, and you want them to be willing then too.

Now you'll be able to relax.

Follow the perfect follow-up game plan and you'll win the play-offs. The reward: the job that's just right for you. Enjoy!

Endnotes

Chapter 4

1. Figure 4.1 is adapted from *How to Turn an Interview into a Job* by Jeffrey G. Allen, J.D., C.P.C.

Chapter 5

1. *The Perfect Job Reference* by Jeffrey G. Allen, J.D., C.P.C.
2. *The Perfect Job Reference* by Jeffrey G. Allen, J.D., C.P.C.
3. *The Perfect Job Reference* by Jeffrey G. Allen, J.D., C.P.C.
4. *The Perfect Job Reference* by Jeffrey G. Allen, J.D., C.P.C.

Chapter 6

1. *Winning Through Intimidation* by Robert J. Ringer.
2. *The Perfect Job Reference* by Jeffrey G. Allen, J.D., C.P.C.
3. *The Perfect Job Reference* by Jeffrey G. Allen, J.D., C.P.C.

4. *How to Turn an Interview into a Job* by Jeffrey G. Allen, J.D., C.P.C.

5. *Psycho-Cybernetics* by Maxwell Maltz.

6. *The Perfect Job Reference* by Jeffrey G. Allen, J.D., C.P.C.

Chapter 7

1. *Closing on Objections* by Paul A. Hawkinson.

2. *How to Turn an Interview into a Job* by Jeffrey G. Allen, J.D., C.P.C.

3. Questions and answers adapted from *How to Turn an Interview into a Job* by Jeffrey G. Allen, J.D., C.P.C.

Chapter 9

1. *The Employee Termination Handbook* by Jeffrey G. Allen, J.D., C.P.C.

2. *Perks and Parachutes* by John Tarrant.

3. *Surviving Corporate Downsizing* by Jeffrey G. Allen, J.D., C.P.C.

4. *The Perfect Job Reference* by Jeffrey G. Allen, J.D., C.P.C.

Appendix

Resources for More Winning Techniques

This book promised ten "Rs" to follow for job-seeking success:

- Review
- Record
- Respond
- Regroup
- Recontact
- Replay
- Realize
- Renegotiate
- Require
- Relax

This section offers a bonus "R": resources that can provide you with additional specialized techniques for your job hunt.

Since the focus of this volume has been on follow-up, the resources here that expand on other aspects of the job search may have particular value.

GENERAL RESOURCES

Allen, James. *As a Man Thinketh*. Marina del Rey, CA: Devorss & Co., 1959.

Allen, Jeffrey G., J.D., C.P.C. *The Employee Termination Handbook*. New York: John Wiley & Sons, 1986.

Allen, Jeffrey G., J.D., C.P.C. *Surviving Corporate Downsizing*. New York: John Wiley & Sons, 1988.

Allen, Jeffrey G., J.D., C.P.C., and Jess Gorkin. *Finding the Right Job at Midlife*. New York: John Wiley & Sons, 1989.

Benson, Herbert, M.D., with Miriam Z. Klipper. *The Relaxation Response*. New York: Avon Books, 1976.

Blake, Robert R., and Jane S. Mouton. *Executive Achievement*. New York: McGraw-Hill, 1986.

Bolles, Richard N. *What Color Is Your Parachute?* Berkeley, CA: Ten Speed Press, 1982.

Fast, Julius. *Body Language*. New York: Pocket Books, 1982.

Forem, Jack. *Transcendental Meditation*. New York: E. P. Dutton, 1973.

Friedman, Thomas. *Up the Ladder: Coping with the Corporate Climb*. New York: Warner Books, 1986.

Heller, Robert. *The Supermanagers*. New York: E. P. Dutton, 1984.

Hill, Napoleon, Ph.D. *Think and Grow Rich*. New York: Random House-Fawcett Books, 1986.

Korda, Michael. *Success!* New York: Ballantine Books, 1978.

Korn, Errol R., M.D., and George J. Pratt, Ph.D., with Peter T.

Lambrou. *Hyper-Performance.* New York: John Wiley & Sons, 1987.

Laureau, William. *Conduct Expected: The Unwritten Rules for a Successful Business Career.* Piscataway, NJ: New Century Publishers, Inc., 1985.

Lee, Nancy. *Targeting the Top.* New York: Doubleday, 1980.

Ringer, Robert J. *Looking Out for Number One.* New York: Fawcett Crest Books, 1978.

Robert, Cavett. *Success with People Through Human Engineering and Motivation.* Chicago: Success Unlimited, 1969.

Tebbetts, Charles. *Self-Hypnosis and Other Mind Expanding Techniques.* Glendale, CA: Westwood Publishing, 1980.

Tec, Leon. *Targets: How to Set Goals for Yourself and Reach Them.* New York: Harper & Row, 1980.

Thain, Richard J. *The Mid-Career Manual.* Englewood Cliffs, NJ: Prentice-Hall, 1982.

Waitley, Denis E., Ph.D. *The Psychology of Winning.* Chicago: Nightingale-Conant, 1979.

Weiss, Allen. *The Organization Guerilla.* New York: Atheneum, 1975.

Ziglar, Zig. *See You at the Top.* Gretna, LA: Pelican Publishing Co., 1983.

JOB-SEARCH RESOURCES

Cole, Kenneth J. *The Headhunter Strategy.* New York: John Wiley & Sons, 1985.

Connaroe, Richard R. *Executive Search.* New York: Van Nostrand Reinhold, 1976.

Freedman, Howard S. *How to Get a Headhunter to Call.* New York: John Wiley & Sons, 1989.

Holtz, Herman. *How to Succeed as an Independent Consultant.* New York: John Wiley & Sons, 1982.

RESUME, REFERENCE, AND COVER LETTER RESOURCES

Allen, Jeffrey G., J.D., C.P.C. *Jeff Allen's Best: The Resume.* New York: John Wiley & Sons, 1990.

Allen, Jeffrey G., J.D., C.P.C. *The Perfect Job Reference.* New York: John Wiley & Sons, 1990.

Beatty, Richard H. *The Perfect Cover Letter.* New York: John Wiley & Sons. 1989.

INTERVIEW RESOURCES

Allen, Jeffrey G., J.D., C.P.C. *The Complete Q&A Job Interview Book.* New York: John Wiley & Sons, 1989.

Allen, Jeffrey G., J.D., C.P.C. *How to Turn an Interview into a Job.* New York: Simon & Schuster, 1981.

Allen, Jeffrey G., J.D., C.P.C. *Jeff Allen's Best: Get the Interview.* New York: John Wiley & Sons, 1990.

Andre, Raye, Ph.D., and Peter J. Ward, J.D. *The 59-Second Employee.* Boston: Houghton Mifflin, 1984.

Hawkinson, Paul A. *Closing on Objections.* St. Louis MO: The Kinberly Organization, 1983. (Order directly from the publisher: P.O. Box 31011, St. Louis, MO 63131. Enclose check for $25.00.)

Molloy, John T. *Dress for Success.* New York: Warner Books, 1975.

Molloy, John T. *The Woman's Dress for Success Book.* New York: Warner Books, 1978.

O'Leary, Lawrence. *Interviewing for the Decision Maker.* Chicago: Nelson Hall, Inc., 1976.

Smart, Bradford D., Ph.D. *The Smart Interviewer: Tools and Techniques for Hiring the Best.* New York: John Wiley & Sons, 1989.

Zunin, Leonard, M.D., with Natalie Zunin. *Contact: The First Four Minutes.* New York: Ballantine Books, 1973.

FOLLOW-UP RESOURCES

Chapman, Jack. *How to Make $1,000 a Minute: Negotiating Salaries & Raises.* Berkeley, CA: Ten Speed Press, 1987.

Cohen, Herb. *You Can Negotiate Anything.* New York: Bantam Books, 1980.

Gould, Richard. *Sacked! Why Good People Get Fired and How to Avoid It.* New York: John Wiley & Sons, 1986.

Hawkinson, Paul A., and Jeffrey G. Allen, J.D., C.P.C. *The Placement Strategy Handbook.* Los Angeles, CA: Search Research Institute, 1985. (Order directly from the publisher: P.O. Box 34343, Los Angeles, CA 90034. Enclose check for $32.50.)

Irish, Richard K. *Go Hire Yourself an Employer.* New York: Doubleday, 1987.

Kennedy, Marilyn Moats. *Salary Strategies.* New York: Bantam Books, 1982.

Kingsley, Daniel T. *How to Fire an Employee.* New York: Facts on File, 1983.

Maltz, Maxwell, M.D., F.I.C.S. *Psycho-Cybernetics.* New York: Pocket Books, 1983.

Nierenberg, Gerald I. *The Complete Negotiator.* New York: Nierenberg & Zief, 1986.

Ringer, Robert J. *Winning Through Intimidation.* New York: Fawcett Crest Books, 1973.

Tarrant, John. *Perks and Parachutes.* New York: Simon & Schuster, 1985.

Uris, Auren, and Jack Tarrant. *How to Keep from Getting Fired.* Chicago: Regnery Co., 1975.

Warschaw, Tessa Albert. *Winning Through Negotiation.* New York: McGraw Hill, 1980.

Woodward, Harvey, Ph.D., and Steve Buchholz, Ph.D. *Aftershock: Helping People Through Corporate Change.* Karen M. Hess, editor. New York: John Wiley & Sons, 1987.

Index